KU-078-966

Tony Byrne

Airlift to Biafra
Breaching the Blockade

the columba press

First published in 1997 by
the columba press
55a Spruce Avenue, Stillorgan Industrial Park,
Blackrock, Co Dublin

Cover by Bill Bolger
Origination by The Columba Press
Printed in Ireland by
Colour Books Ltd, Dublin
ISBN 185607 201 0

Copyright © 1997, Tony Byrne

Contents

Nigeria and the Gulf of Guinea

Foreword

To those under forty today, the word Biafra may only evoke a question mark. For those a mite older the word will jog a chord of memory, for the thirty-month war between The Federal Republic of Nigeria and its former Eastern Province became one of the most emotive causes of the latter half of this century.

For those intimately involved in the fighting and the suffering, it remains a scar that will never fade.

Basically, the people of Eastern Nigeria decided by overwhelming majority in July 1967 that they could no longer accept the thralldom of the military junta in the federal capital and declared separate independence under the ancient title of Biafra. What followed, supposedly a ten-day operation to re-unify the country of Nigeria, was a two-and-a-half year calvary for the minority ethnic group who, though defeated in the end, wrote their name by courage and pain into the pages of history.

Biafra established several 'firsts'. One was that it became the first mass-starvation of men, women and children in Africa to reach the people of Western Europe and North America in all its horror by the medium of television. Ethiopia, Somalia and Sudan came later.

The effect of these television images of children reduced to walking skeletons was profound on those who had never seen such things. Towards the crisis poured a welter of outsiders trying to help, or just help themselves: politicians, journalists, cameramen, philanthropists, doctors, pilots and pundits; along with mercenaries, arms dealers, oilmen, con-men and call-girls. No author could have invented such a cast-list.

The other oddity about Biafra was this: because the establishments and therefore governments of the West, the Soviet bloc and the Third World opposed 'rebels' in principle, they all supported the Lagos government, corrupt and militaristic dictatorship though it might be. Ordinary people, disgusted by the sufferings they saw, in great majority supported the breakaway young state of Biafra.

The result was that any aid reaching the dying children was devoid of official backing, something that has never happened before or since.

Deprived of governmental facilities, the task of trying to keep the dying children of Biafra alive while the fighting raged, was taken up by the churches. Apart from the secular International Red Cross, these were the mainly Protestant World Council of Churches and the Catholic Caritas Internationalis, co-operating under the title of Joint Church Aid.

At the very heart of the vortex was a group of Catholic and Protestant missionaries, with their local colleagues, women and men who but for the war would probably have continued in humble and anonymous pastoral work among their people until called away by age, infirmity or God.

But strange events often produce the needed people. Some remained inside the fighting enclave, shepherding their flocks away from the firing lines, running the feeding centres, refugee homes and orphanages, tending the sick, giving interviews to the ever-hungry TV crews, appealing for help, distributing relief food and giving many, many Last Rites.

Others struggled in a more international role, flitting in and out of the Biafran enclave as the Nigerian food-blockade tightened its grip, organising the great airlift in which freelance pilots flying from offshore islands brought in thousands of tons of baby-milk and food concentrates by night to a secret airstrip cut from the bush, or pleading their case in the chancelleries of the Vatican, Rome, Paris, London, Dublin and Washington.

Thirty years on, newly released papers show how frustrated the authorities became that the Biafrans would not surrender or lie down and die quietly; that the press would not stop releasing their terrible images and reports; and that the missionaries and their helpers would not stop rocking the diplomatic boat. These papers were written by plump white hands, of men on plump white bottoms, who had never heard the rattle of machine guns between the palms, the crack of mortar in a crowded village square, the singing hiss of an incoming bomb nor the whimper of a dying child.

Biafra too died. On 10 January, 1970, after thirty months of struggle that defied the experts and the official world. Yet there remains a memorial to those of all colours and creeds who tried to help.

It is not cast in stone, nor yet of bronze. It walks and breathes. It is the half a million Biafran children who, at a reasoned estimate, would have died of hunger and malnutrition but for the airlift and the brought-in food, but who today are in their thirties, married, with children of their own.

Most of these will never have heard his name, yet among the most effective 'fixers' of the airlift, of the food and famine relief programme in those years, was the one his exasperated opponents in high places called the Green Pimpernel. Father Tony Byrne. This is his story.

Frederick Forsyth
Hertford, 1997

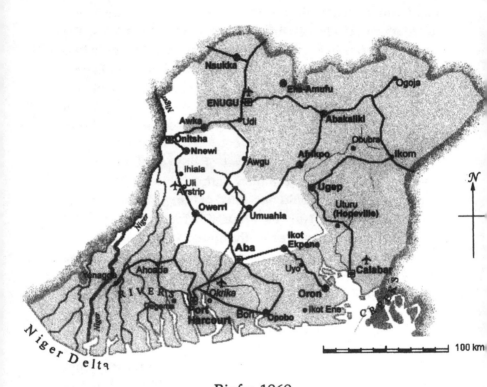

Biafra 1969

When Biafra seceded, 14 million Biafrans lived in the area of the full map. By 1969, Nigerian forces had retaken most of the country and 11 million were confined to the small area shown in white.

Prologue

Biafra
December 1969

Anxious faces stared at each other in silence. No one wanted to express feelings, no one dared state the obvious, as a crescendo of lethal sound filled the air, paralysing everyone with fear at the airstrip.

Shells could be heard everywhere, their constant whining tearing at our nerves. Heavier sounds came from the bombers, as they pounded the nearby villages. Most terrifying of all, though, were the tell-tale sights and sounds of the rockets from the MiGs and the tanks.

All this was just the overture, a carefully planned 'softening-up' operation preparing the way for the final onslaught on Biafra. The Biafrans' response of sporadic machine-gun fire would be easily brushed aside by the military might of the advancing Nigerian army.

In the meantime, Uli 'airport' remained operational.

The DC 7 was almost ready, its load of stockfish and salt already spirited away to where it was needed. The three Americans who would fly it were chatting earnestly nearby as they waited for clearance. They were about to fly me to our base at São Tomé, a beautiful island just four hundred miles away. There, we would take on a full load of fuel before flying to Lisbon.

Captain Henry Turner wore his customary tropical uniform – a pale yellow open-neck shirt and blue bermuda shorts. His young co-pilot, Skip McVitie, was equally informal but the older engineer, Larry Carter, wore a uniform shirt – proudly displaying a single wing.

Henry looked tense but confident. His long experience of combat flying in Vietnam was a good preparation for the dangerous flight he was about to make. He seemed completely calm as he called me aside and tried to prepare me for the dangers ahead:

'I guess you know the score, Tony. Fighting near the airstrip... too damn close for comfort... I'll lift the aircraft fast... get above most of the flak... all lights off. Stay cool, man, and with a bit of luck we'll make it. OK, let's go!'

As I followed him into the relief aircraft, the bombardment mounted and thickened, both in noise and in power, some miles away. I tried to imagine that the quivering in my legs was caused by the rickety makeshift ladder and I envied the studied nonchalance of the others.

When I sat down, these feelings were soon overpowered by the thought of leaving behind the many close friends I had made during my ten years here. Would I ever see them again? My God, what would happen to them? Would they survive the onslaught of the Nigerian army? Or starve to death?

These thoughts, in turn, were pushed aside by the roar of the engines as we raced down the runway. It seemed impossible that anything could get through the maelstrom of tracer and shellbursts, but soon the engines were just groaning as Henry lifted the aircraft safely clear of it all.

The unpleasant smell of dried stockfish, which had been off-loaded from the plane in Biafra, haunted the air in the cabin. It was like the poignant smell of decaying corpses. In an uncanny way, it seemed to echo what was happening some two thousand feet below. I looked out the window at the crumbling nation now shrinking into oblivion beneath me. There was no hope for it now. This young breakaway State of Biafra was slowly bleeding to death. It was a battle lost and yet, in a certain sense, a battle won.

The Biafrans had won the propaganda war of the foreign affairs mandarins and the military experts. These 'experts' had forecast that Biafra would hold out against the powerful, internationally supported, Nigerian army for a week or two. In their ponderous predictions they had scoffed, saying that this war would be a storm in a tea-cup, a mere skirmish. One sharp strike by the Nigerian forces would be sufficient to suppress the badly equipped Biafran rebel soldiers. These pundits had been gazing into the wrong military crystal ball for the past two-and-a-half years. Biafra was still there.

The DC 7 levelled off at its maximum cruising altitude and the sky around us filled with flashes of green and red tracers from the Nigerian anti-aircraft guns. The vivid colours seemed even more terrifying set against the dark night sky but luckily, the gunners were off-target. Henry made several rapid course changes to confuse them and we were soon clear.

The horrific memory of what I had seen and experienced during the past few days in Biafra replaced my fears. Those haunting sights would never leave me. The dead and dying lying everywhere on the streets. The cries of the starving children, the frightening din of exploding shells and rockets and the hopelessness reflected in the sunken faces of hungry, displaced people. They had moved from one refugee camp to another, trying to avoid the advancing Nigerian army. Now their country was reduced to a small enclave, leaving them nowhere to run, nowhere to escape.

The frightened face of a young boy-soldier lying motionless on an army truck, both legs blown off, was vivid in my mind. I had given him the Last Rites, but beyond that, all I could do was hold his hands as he died. There were other soldiers, too, fleeing from the war-front, throwing off their uniforms from their half-starved bodies, mingling with civilians, hoping to lose their identity.

Thinking of the root cause of this bitter war – the rich oil resources of Biafra – made me fume with anger. This war might never have happened if those resources were not there. No one need have died.

My anger deepened as I thought of the countries that had

unscrupulously sold or donated military hardware to Nigeria and Biafra. The rockets that had just terrified us at Uli had come from Russian-supplied MiG fighters and British-donated tanks. The bombers, too, had been supplied by Russia. These countries used armaments for their own economic or political gain at the expense of the lives of many innocent people. No! No innocents need have been sacrificed to these modern cults of oil and greed.

Captain Turner's voice on the public address system distracted me temporarily from these bitter feelings:

'Tony, fasten your seat-belt now. We're just passing Port Harcourt and running into some nasty turbulence. It never lasts long.'

The turbulence tossed the empty aircraft like a leaf in the wind. The weather matched my mood. Psychologically, I felt part of that turbulence as I experienced doubts about my own role. Was it a waste of time going to Rome, now? Was I running away from the tragic situation in Biafra? Was I abandoning ship, taking the easy option?

Even more disturbing questions went through my mind about my personal life. Was this the priestly way of life I had voluntarily taken on? Was I properly trained and prepared? Is it possible to be adequately prepared for life's experiences of joys and sorrows, challenges and risks?

The turbulence outside passed, but not the one within me. Many questions remained unanswered, puzzling me.

Henry left the controls to Skip and came back to me in the cabin. We were well clear of Port Harcourt, the turbulence already forgotten, the Biafran coast behind us and just 250 miles of sea and sky between us and São Tomé.

There were only two passenger seats on these aircraft. Henry sat down beside me. It was a few moments before he spoke:

'Well Tony, it looks like curtains for Biafra. This milk run is drawing to a close. I'm afraid it won't be possible to fly relief supplies to Uli much longer.'

I nodded.

'What will happen to those poor kids in Biafra? How will they get food? Something should be done to save their lives. God, we can't leave them starving to death. It's not right. Tony, what about an air-drop of supplies?'

'We'll have to think about that and see what can be done.'

Henry eyed me with disappointment and returned to the cockpit.

His questions made me feel awful. I was on my way to Rome to make a personal appeal for permission for just such a drop. I had a genuine respect for Henry and desperately wanted to tell him the real purpose of my journey. But what could I tell him? In the face of the carnage we had just seen, how could I tell him that I was far from confident about the appeal?

Like most of the pilots, Henry genuinely cared about the Biafran children. To him they were real people, not statistics. He had lifted many of them in his arms, hugged and re-assured them as he ferried them to and from hospital.

How could I explain to him that I had already tried and failed to organise an air-drop? How could I expect him to understand how the church operates, when I scarcely under-stood the diplomatic considerations myself? I couldn't explain the bureaucratic elements in detail, either.

That would be disloyal.

* * *

São Tomé was the base used by the churches for flying relief supplies to Biafra. Some months before, an aid organisation had sent 8,000 parachutes to São Tomé in case they would be needed for an airdrop. As director of the Catholic Church relief programme to Biafra, I had asked Rome for permission to use them if it became impossible to land our aircraft at Uli.

Monsignor Carlo Bayer, chief of the Vatican relief organisation, Caritas Internationalis, cabled the official reply: 'Sorry, the Vatican regards parachutes as quasi-military equipment. We are strictly forbidden to use them. I am afraid we have no choice in this matter. Forget your plans for the proposed air-drop. Greetings, Bayer.'

This decision infuriated me. I was sure it wasn't Bayer's doing – that would be out of character. It sounded much more like the thinking of those highly trained Vatican officials who tended to allow diplomacy to take precedence over all other considerations. However difficult it might be to persuade them, I was determined to do all I could to have the policy reversed.

When we reached Lisbon, I would take the first available commercial flight to Rome. There, I would argue that the parachutes were the only way to save innocent lives now. I was determined to make the most personal and passionate appeal I possibly could.

* * *

Colonel Chukwuemeka Odumegwu Ojukwu, the Head of the secessionist Biafran State, was a courteous and approachable man. I had met him several times but yesterday's meeting, to request him to support my appeal, was quite different. As usual, it was arranged formally through some Igbo friends.

The State House was always in danger of being bombed and strafed by Nigerian MiGs. It had to be camouflaged with palm leaves to avoid detection from the air. After many security checks, an army officer led me into a large blue-carpeted room, sparsely furnished with four carved chairs and small coffee tables. One chair was padded in red velvet. The officer pointed to it. 'His Excellency will sit there.'

After a short time, Ojukwu entered the room, greeted me warmly in his attractive voice, soft and reassuring. His well-tailored uniform was handsomely decorated. Looking relaxed, he stroked his bushy beard carefully.

I had expected to meet a nervous military Head of State,

disquieted by the deteriorating military situation under his command. Instead, he was the serene commander, almost blissfully happy, in full control of his emotions as a soldier served cold drinks. Taking a deep breath, I smiled and tried to pick my words carefully as I addressed him formally:

'Your Excellency, I've come to ask for your advice and assistance. You are aware that our church relief organisations in São Tomé have sixteen relief planes and a considerable stock-pile of food and medicines in our warehouses. Caritas also has 8,000 parachutes which were donated in case an emergency airdrop might prove necessary. Unfortunately, the Vatican forbids Catholic relief organisations to use them because they are considered to be quasi-military equipment.'

Ojukwu flashed his eyes, plucked his beard and shuffled uneasily.

'As you know, Uli airstrip is quite near the war-front now. If the Nigerians get any closer to it, our pilots may no longer be willing to use it. That would make the airlift impossible to continue. Since food and medicines are critically scarce all over the country, I plan to leave Biafra tomorrow for the Vatican to appeal for clearance to use the parachutes. It would be most helpful if you would support that appeal.'

Ojukwu stared at me intently for a few moments. His penetrating brown eyes unnerved me, as he breathed hard through his nose. He slowly heaved himself out of his seat, stood erect, placed his hands behind his back and stalked up and down the room in deadly silence. He stood still for a moment, his eyes riveted on me. His voice was slow and determined.

'Father Byrne, I have maximum confidence in the gallant Biafran troops.'

His face was mottling with rage. He bade me farewell with formal courtesy, then he abruptly left the room.

I was dismissed.

It was obvious that I had upset him. But how? Was he unaware of the situation? That seemed impossible and yet his reaction was understandable only if he had not understood the reality of the military situation outside. Perhaps I had made him realise that his dream of an internationally recognised State of Biafra was about to end. Perhaps, for the first time, he had become fully aware of the possible demise of Biafra.

* * *

Henry's voice broke through my thoughts again: 'Hi, Tony, we made it. We will be landing in São Tomé in about twenty minutes. I'm going to take-off again as quickly as possible. Can you stay with the plane while we refuel?'

Of course, I had met many pilots returning from the relief flights into Uli. 'We made it,' seemed to be the first thing they said – every time. The stress and strain showing in their eyes always denied their boyish grins. I didn't have to see Henry to know his face would show that same mixture of strain and relief as he tried to sound businesslike on the intercom.

When Henry came back to me, I told him I would be delighted to stay in the plane. I didn't bother him with my real reason. If the international media in São Tomé even suspected why I was going to the Vatican, the resultant publicity would not be appreciated there.

Yes, a quick take-off would suit everyone!

CHAPTER 1

Too Hot for Pyjamas

It was getting near midnight as we approached the island. As usual, the first thing that struck me were the lights. Nothing special, but they were switched *on*, in stark contrast to the situation in Biafra. They seemed to wink reassuringly at us, confirming that there were no MiGs to worry about here. Another world.

São Tomé is beautiful. Known as Paradise Island, its 7,000 square kilometres are bounded by far-stretching golden beaches and overlooked by stunningly beautiful wooded mountains. It should have been thronged with tourists but most of the 60,000 Africans and Portuguese who lived there had to survive by growing coffee and cocoa.

To its Portuguese masters, this was a prison island and a strategic base. Visitors were not welcome. Against a backdrop of such beauty, it was hard to believe that Africans and their supporters were being tortured in the island's jail. Yet the accusations were too widespread to be dismissed.

Its location and air facilities made São Tomé an ideal base for the churches' relief airlift to Biafra. For nearly two years the relief planes had been flying practically every night from the island and from Libreville, the capital of Gabon – 300 kilometres to the east.

At first, the flights were straightforward – 500 kilometres due north from the island to Port Harcourt on the Biafran coast. When Port Harcourt fell, the dangers increased as the church aircraft had to fly beyond it to Uli airstrip. But they were still short flights, needing little fuel, so that each aircraft could be laden with the precious cargoes of stockfish, maize and, of course, salt. With these bulky cargoes, the equation was quite simple – each extra pound of fuel needed meant a pound less cargo. It seemed strange, then, to watch Henry's plane take on a full load of fuel with no cargo.

As soon as the fuel was loaded, Henry went off to deal with the paperwork. Skip and I stretched our legs on a short walk beside the aircraft. He explained that the flight to Lisbon would take about fourteen hours and that the route would be somewhat unusual in order to stay well clear of Nigeria.

Shortly after we took off, Larry arrived with two cans of Coke:

'Coffee's rather awkward on these DC 7s, Tony, slightly un-official and strictly rationed. I'll heat some up later, but would you try a soda?'

'Anything with sugar in it would be great.'

For weeks, hardly anyone in Biafra had sugar. What little there was, had been kept for the smaller children. The sugary mineral, or 'soda' as Larry called it, seemed like a special treat.

He looked at me sympathetically:

'I hope you won't be too lonely. I guess it must feel strange to be the only passenger on a fourteen-hour flight.'

'Don't worry, I've a lot to think about.'

Larry peered out the windows to check his engines and then sat beside me. He lit a king-size filter cigarette and drew on it for a moment. Then he ran his hands through his wild, crinkly red hair and murmured:

'Of course, a 707 *could* do it in four-and-a-half hours. The last 707 I was on had Rolls Royce engines. Real beauties. Have you ever flown on one?'

'Yes, Larry, but even the DC 7 is a lot faster than the *Tarkwa*!'

'The *Tarkwa*?'

'The SS *Tarkwa* was the elderly steamer that brought me to Nigeria the first time. It took three weeks, straining to maintain twelve knots.'

'Wow! I've never been on a steamer. You must tell me about

her the next break I get. Did you get to see the engines? Were they enormous?'

'Two of them. Each as big as the fuselage of a DC 7.'

* * *

The SS *Tarkwa* was, as her crew affectionately described her, a lady whose dashing days were over. Even in ideal conditions, she was sorely pressed to maintain her cruising speed of twelve knots – in stark contrast to the speed at which the DC 7 raced along, some 230 knots, I believe Skip said.

Sixteen of us joined the *Tarkwa* in Liverpool for the voyage to Port Harcourt, in Nigeria. For most of us, it was our first missionary assignment. We were full of enthusiasm, just recently ordained priests and keen to put into practice everything we had learnt, the Novice Master's admonition that we should be 'men for all seasons' fresh in our minds.

It was also our first long voyage by ship. At first, the crew answered our questions with bemused tolerance, patiently explaining the sea's strange terminology. By the time we had cleared the Bay of Biscay, though, we had found our sea-legs and knew our port from starboard, our forrard from aft.

The *Tarkwa* was one of a dying breed, typical of another age when Britain had many colonies to service. She was a cargo ship with space for a limited number of passengers, designed to carry goods and administrators in both directions. Now most of her trade was with the emergent, new nations of Africa – many of them former British colonies.

Her passengers, too, still included colonial administrators – and many more who still thought of themselves as such. The new nations of Africa still needed their technical and administrative experience, but it was obvious that they still had to come to terms with the changing realities of the continent. No proud young nation would tolerate, for long, people who used derogatory terms like 'natives'. I doubted if many could make the necessary changes.

Meals in the dining room were shared with people whose conversation seemed to focus on the 'natives'. The prejudice

of some of these frustrated colonists was breathtaking in its
arrogance and made tiresome conversation. The wife of a
District Officer in Nigeria was typical of many:

'Reverend, may I be bold enough to give you some words
of advice. You're a young man with no African experience.
I've worked in Nigeria for more than twenty years and I
know that one can't trust the natives. If one does so, one can
be frightfully disappointed. Even the best of them can steal
all sorts of things. One must be careful with them. It's so hard
to get them to work. They're extremely lazy people.'

Thankfully, what she and others told me has been proven to
be untrue. My ten years' experience of working with
Nigerians was a wonderfully positive one, learning and sharing experiences in friendship and mutual respect.

The weeks on the *Tarkwa* were a break for us, a respite that
helped us to make the transition from the scholastic world
that had dominated our lives for the past seven years. Like all
young people, we wanted to make changes, improvements, put
our own stamp on things.

As students in Ireland, local church laws had obliged us to
wear black suits, clerical collars and black hats. Clerical attire
was understandable for church services, but I detested wearing it at other times. The black hat, in particular, struck me as
an elitist symbol and I wondered if others felt the same way.

Four of us shared a cabin, well aft on the ship. One morning in the Bay of Biscay, Dick Brophy called us:

'I've had a peek outside, lads, and it looks like a great morning for a hat-throwing. Shall we say 9.30 after breakfast, upper
deck, port side?'

The bunk above me groaned as Gerry Smith, our gentle
giant who was happier squeezing into the second row of a
rugby scrum than this cramped berth, propped himself on an
elbow:

'They tell me the French like hats. They can have mine!'

'Anybody can have mine.'

'And mine.'

Not another word seemed to be spoken about hats but, by 9.30, more than a dozen of us lined up on the upper deck. One by one, with great ceremony, we tossed our hats into the rough sea, in the direction of France.

The *Tarkwa*'s British Captain, Norman Wilson, was a professional seaman with an impeccable record. Although he wasn't tall, he had a commanding presence. He set high standards and the crew willingly followed him.

On a rota basis, the Captain invited passengers to dine with him at his table, usually followed by drinks in the lounge. Over these drinks, he often made silly remarks about the Irish. Normally, these were easily overlooked. The day England beat Ireland at rugby, however, the Captain went too far! He was exultant, telling everyone how England had been 'too hot' for Ireland and putting the score on his notice-board adding: 'Ireland, RIP.'

That got Joe Regan's dander up and he suggested to Nick Carey, the ship's Irish electrician, that they needed a confab over a pint – and 'it might even be a two-pint job. It seems the Captain doesn't understand the Irish, Nick. Do you think we might help the poor chap improve his sensitivity?'

'A noble cause, Joe. A noble cause... but it might be a lost one, too. He's a great Captain but the whole crew are fed up with this thing, not just the Irish. They say it's gone on since his student days. He may not be able to change.'

'We've got to try. He kept going on about the English being 'too hot' for us. Is there anything we could do with heat?'

'That's my department! The radiator in his cabin might get stuck on maximum or his air-conditioning could malfunction...'

'How about both?'

'A bit drastic, Joe.'

'This needs to be drastic!'

They were both chuckling now and, by the time the second pint had come and gone, it was all planned. Nick might be suspected of adjusting the equipment, but it was the work of a moment to arrange for one of the other Irish crewmen to do it – while they continued to establish their alibi:

'Could we have two more pints, please?'

The following morning, Joe was up bright and early and made sure he arrived for breakfast at the same time as the Captain.

'Good morning, Captain. What a beautiful day!'

'Er, yes, padre. A lovely morning. I trust you slept well.'

'An excellent night, Captain. Your ship's air-conditioning is wonderful.'

He dropped his voice before adding, confidentially:

'With such luxury, I can't understand people complaining that their cabins are too hot.'

The voyage to Nigeria involved a short stop-over in Freetown, Sierra Leone. While we were docked in Freetown, young men paddled their canoes alongside the ship and shouted up to us: 'You like some fruit? They're fine. Sweet ones. Get a rope and bucket. Send us down some money and we'll send you back some fruit.'

They had pineapples, paw-paw, oranges, grapefruit and mangoes. We had no local currency but that didn't stop Joe. Unabashed, he shouted: 'Sorry, we've no money. If we send down soap, will you give us some fruit?'

'Yes sir, OK, fine.'

We quickly gathered soap from the cabins and sent it down in a bucket. The young canoe men filled the bucket with fruit, delighted with the perfumed soap of the ship. A little later Joe brought a dish of fruit to the Captain's cabin. When the Captain opened the door he raised his eyebrows in surprise:

'Padre, what is this?'

Joe blinked, cleared his throat and grinned:

'A small token of our friendship and appreciation, Captain.'

The Captain thought for a moment, then took the dish of fruit in his hands. His eyes crinkled in a smile: 'Padre, you're very kind. It's always a privilege having you Irish missionaries on board. Why don't you join me for a drink.'

As he poured their second drink, Wilson casually murmured: 'Some passengers prefer a less scented soap than the
one we normally use. I was thinking of changing it. What do
you think, padre?'

'I think you don't miss much, Captain!'

'A Captain shouldn't miss *anything*, padre!'

When we arrived at Port Harcourt, we bade goodbye to each
other, to the crew and to our fellow passengers. Although we
were excited at the thought of our respective missions, we
were surprised at the strength of the friendships we had
made on the three-week voyage.

Seasoned missionaries met us on board. Tom O'Mahony
introduced himself and told me that I was appointed to
Aguleri parish, where he would be my parish priest. I tried
not to be too obvious as I studied him carefully. This man,
who was to be my superior and mentor in missionary work,
looked rather daunting. Tall and well-built, his expressive
face and steel-grey eyes reflected strength and determination.
In one glance, I noted his grey tropical helmet and the long
off-white cassock. The cassock was tied in the middle with a
black cincture, whose tassels almost touched the ground.

After a perfunctory search by customs officials, the two tin
boxes packed with my belongings were tied on the roof-rack
of an old Volkswagen Beetle and we set off on the long journey to Aguleri. When we were a short time on the road I asked
casually: 'What's it like in Aguleri, Tom? Is it in the bush?'

'Well my young man, now that you ask me, perhaps you
should know the truth. The mission you're going to is in a
very remote area and is regarded as the toughest parish in the
Archdiocese. The mission house is reputed to be haunted and
your predecessor, Fr Joe Delaney, suffered from leprosy. I'm
sure you heard of his death before you left Ireland.'

I tried to look composed, a 'man for all seasons', as I had
been trained to do! He was just being honest, breaking me in
the hard way, I hoped!

When we arrived at the mission house in Aguleri, Tom garaged the car. I was stiff and tired from the long journey in the uncomfortable Volkswagen. It was six-thirty, almost totally dark, but the faint evening light was pleasant after so much burning sunshine. As we walked from the garage towards the mission house we stopped for a few moments, looking down the hill to a small village nearby. As the light became fainter and fainter, we could see oil lamps burning outside huts where women sold cola nuts and roasted corn.

Then Tom gestured me to a grave near the entrance to the mission house. It was decorated with artificial flowers and surrounded with whitewashed stones. It had a black wooden cross at its head. Tom beckoned to me to pray:

'This is the grave of poor Joseph Delaney. He suffered a lot from leprosy. The local people in Aguleri regard him as a saint.'

After that, I looked in silence for a while at my future home. Its brick walls were whitewashed and it was roofed with red zinc sheets. The window frames were fitted with mosquito mesh. It looked austere and uninviting. Inside, the furniture was old and stained.

When I walked on the bare wooden floor in the sitting room, the boards creaked noisily. There was no electricity. Oil lamps gave a shadowed light and burned the mosquitoes and flies that flew into their flames. From time to time, bats flew blindly around the rooms, dotting them with their droppings and adding to the smells. The high temperature and torturous humidity made my skin prickly. The perspiration ran down my chest in rivulets. A trickle of water from the shower in the bathroom did little to freshen me.

Tom offered me a whiskey and a lukewarm soda from the kerosene fridge. When I told him I'd prefer a Coke, he said: 'In this country, my young man, it's either Punch or Judy. I advise you to stay with the punch. You must be careful. If you drink water that isn't boiled and filtered you will become very ill. Be careful when you're walking around. This area has lots of deadly snakes. Be sure to use a torch when you're walking at night.'

Later he told me about the financial difficulties in the parish: 'We've more than eighty schools here. The people are very poor and many of them can't pay school-fees. The parish has a big debt and the bank manager isn't happy with the situation.'

Eventually I went to my bedroom feeling lonely, tired and frightened. The bed was old-fashioned. It had steel sides and sagging springs supporting a lumpy mattress. I suspected that it was one of the beds brought by the French missionaries when they first came to the parish in 1892.

A net surrounded the bed but provided no real protection from mosquitoes or other flying creatures that could easily enter through its many holes. The perspiration saturated my pyjamas, sheets and pillow. Bats clawed on the mosquito net and frightened me. Tropical insects hummed and frogs croaked continuously outside, making my first night long and sleepless. I wondered how I'd survive in such a difficult place. I twisted and turned in bed, recalling all the things Tom had told me: the house said to be haunted, leprosy, bankruptcy of the parish, snakes and contaminated water. I shed a few tears as I thought of these difficulties and the home comforts I'd left back in Ireland. However, my admiration for Tom's endurance and zeal challenged me to prove that all my training for missionary work was not in vain.

Next morning he served a very substantial breakfast, although I didn't feel like eating because of the tremendous heat and humidity.

'You must eat well or you won't last long. How did you sleep last night?'

'I didn't sleep at all. It was too warm.'

He replied in his usual outspoken manner: 'You should remember that in this country it's too hot for pyjamas. Sleep with only a sheet over you. However, make sure you have your pyjamas ready in case of a fire.'

* * *

The Anambra was a tributary of the Niger that flowed through Aguleri parish. Tom and I took turns travelling up it in dug-out canoes. Where the river didn't go, we walked. A typical trek lasted two or three weeks – visiting schools and ministering to the people.

On my first trek, I was somewhat nervous and didn't know what to expect. Joseph Okafor was the catechist. He and I travelled by canoe and walked to remote areas where the local people welcomed us warmly. As we walked on a bush path, I noticed large footprints and asked:

'What animal made these?'

'They're elephant tracks. There are many in this area.'

'Are they dangerous? Will they stampede? What should we do if we see them along this path?'

Joseph laughed at my nervousness: 'Don't worry, these elephants don't normally stampede. However, they may be frightened when they see you because you are white. If they stampede, don't run up a tree because they may knock it down. The best thing to do is to run like this.' He drew a zigzag line in the sand: 'Elephants can't run like that.'

On these trips, Joseph and I slept in the school buildings. They had half-walls with wooden posts cemented into them to support the zinc roofs. There were no doors and Joseph always insisted that his camp bed should be nearer than mine to the school entrance. I didn't understand why he was so insistent. Eventually my curiosity made me ask:

'Joseph, every time we reach a school where we sleep, you insist that your bed should be near the entrance. Is there some special reason?'

He hesitated before answering:

'If wild animals enter the school, and you're sleeping away from the entrance, you can escape by jumping over the wall and running away. Priests are scarce.'

I was amazed at his spirit of sacrifice and, in spite of my efforts to sleep near the entrance, Joseph would never let me do so.

One of the ways of whiling away the long hours on the rivers was to pass around a traditional pot, or calabash, of palm wine to the paddlers. The wine encouraged them to sing their local boat songs, entertaining us, and increasing the speed of the canoes as the paddlers pulled with the rhythm of the songs.

There was such a variety in the songs that, at first, I thought they must have come from different tribes. Joseph assured me that they were all from his own tribe, the Igbo (pronounced ee'bo). Different villages just had their favourite songs and their own versions of popular ones.

When Joseph realised that my interest in Igbo culture and traditions was genuine, he became my willing mentor. Patiently, he explained the origins of everything from boat songs and hunting sagas to wedding and harvest dances. Through them he told me the handed-down folklore and history of his people, their complex relationships with the neighbouring tribes and their different customs, cultures and traditions. It was a fascinating way to learn history.

I tried to explain the love-hate relationship we Irish had with the English. The common bonds of our shared history and our similarities ensure that the Irish and the English are not just neighbours, but close friends. At the same time, the characteristic little differences – and the same shared history – can create the flashpoints which drive us apart. Most of the time, I felt that Joseph had an even better understanding of the relationship than I did.

The joy and sense of fulfilment I experienced working with the Igbo people far outweighed the hardships I endured. Their positive approach to the difficulties of life made me see my problems from a different perspective. Even though they had few of this world's comforts, a smile was never far from their faces. They taught me far more than I taught them, especially about relationships and community living. Their sharp intelligence, willingness to learn, and their respect for the aged endeared them to me.

* * *

It took some time to adjust to the different circumstances and attitudes in Nigeria. I made assumptions based on my own experience and was often not conscious that I was doing so.

There was a period of seasonal flooding in Aguleri. Water covered the people's mud houses and went as high as the palm trees. During a church service, I sympathised with the people on their suffering and the congregation broke into spontaneous laughter. Joseph came to me, looking embarrassed:

'They were laughing at what you said because flooding isn't a time of suffering for us. In fact, it's a happy time because we can travel in our canoes to see relatives and friends in other villages. Fish is plentiful. When the floods are finished it's easy to make mud blocks to build new houses. The land is very easy to cultivate because the soil is soft for planting.'

Of course, Joseph was right. I watched families travelling happily in their canoes, bringing their possessions with them – yams, goats, sheep and fowl included. It was party time for them, with lots of fish to eat and share as they visited their relatives and friends in the other flooded villages.

I found it very difficult to understand the attitude of local people to time. They might arrive an hour or two late for appointments but those who came late could never understand why I was upset. Then I realised their concept of time was different from mine. For them there was only one time, not three kinds – past, present and future. A Nigerian friend explained it beautifully:

'Europeans have watches, Nigerians have time.'

Although it gave rise to problems and misunderstandings with Europeans, I came to admire much of this philosophy, which didn't recognise the difference between wasting time and spending it.

Time wasn't wasted when people were in personal contact with each other. A local chief made the point succinctly as he made a speech to welcome the bishop to my parish. With

great courtesy and formality, he thanked the bishop 'for sending Father Tony to waste his time working in this parish!'

As I learnt about their traditions, many Igbos were keen to
learn about our European ways, too. New skills were adopted,
others adapted or rejected. The differences, and the ways we
misunderstood them, often gave us a laugh.

Linus Idika was the leader of one of our youth clubs. He
was a born leader, an energetic and popular carpenter, who
dedicated his free time to the youth club. One day, I showed
him the script of a play: 'Linus, do you think the club would
be interested in this play? Would you like to translate it into
Igbo and put on a show in the parish hall?' It was about the
life of St Francis of Assisi and opened with a scene in which
the flamboyant, unconverted Francis was living a wild life and
drinking heavily with his companions in a bar. Their first
song was 'Santa Lucia'.

Linus took the script, flicked through it and stopped to
read some pages carefully, grunting a few times as he read.
Then he looked at me for a few seconds and smiled:

'Hey, I like this thing, it's fine, but we'll have to take out
the white man stuff so that people will understand it. Let me
talk to my members and I'll tell you what they think.'

As Linus left, I wondered if I would hear any more about
the play.

Some weeks later, he called to see me, looking excited:

'Father Tony, that play is good. We've translated it and
changed it a little. Young people have been selected to play
the different roles and have learned their parts. Are you free
on Friday night to see our first dress rehearsal?'

'Well done, Linus. I'm looking forward to it.'

The curtain on the stage opened and a striking Francis
came out, dancing with his companions to the rhythm of
African drums and tambourines. The stage was alive with
movement, music and song as the actors danced around a calabash full of palm wine. They filled their glasses with the palm
wine as they sang, with great gusto:

'Wine is better in the belly, than in the calabash.'

'Santa Lucia' never sounded better.

This was real inculturation. The young people had adapted the play and made it relevant to their own lives and values. Later, they built a portable stage and brought the play to other towns where it was greatly appreciated.

Hospitality in Nigeria is deeply rooted in the local culture. Food is shared and it is rude to ask visitors: 'Are you going to eat?' It is presumed that visitors must eat. When an unexpected visitor arrives during a mealtime they simply say: 'We will split the plate with the visitor.'

I visited Fr William Eke in a neighbouring parish. He was not expecting me but gave me a warm welcome.

'William, I am sorry that I couldn't let you know I was coming.'

He was taken aback by my apology and looked at me in puzzlement:

'Tony, are you my enemy or my friend? Why would you have to tell me that you are coming? There is no need. My people have a proverb that says: "the road has no mouth". We always regard visitors as a blessing.'

There were great changes in the church, too. As everywhere else, services were now celebrated in the local language at a simpler, less ornate altar, closer to the people. Some of the older missionaries struggled with the changes. A young priest was explaining them to a much older priest. An enthusiastic golfer, but not exactly enthusiastic about the changes, the older man grumbled: 'All these changes are too much for me. You would need a caddie with you to say Mass these days.'

Midnight Mass at Christmas was being broadcast from our parish for the first time and it fell to me to provide the radio commentary. Donatus appointed himself my assistant, fascinated by all the strange equipment. It was a delightful, simple ceremony and I was enjoying my first experience as a commentator. During the broadcast, my throat became very dry and I asked Donatus to get me some iced water.

A very elderly bishop got up to preach. It was embarrassing as he spoke at great length of a dying fellow missionary, entirely inappropriate for this Christmas night of great joy. I struggled for words.

As I walked out of the church, I met the radio producer and asked him: 'How did it go? I hope I said the right things.'

'Tony, the broadcast was a fiasco. A young man with a bottle of water tripped over a cable in the dark, the cable to the broadcasting van was disconnected and our electrician had gone for Christmas.'

I exploded: 'Why didn't you tell me we were off the air?'

'Ah, Tony, the ceremony was so beautiful I didn't want to disturb the people in the church.'

* * *

Life in Nigeria was lightened by the sense of humour of the people. Smiles were always abundant. Language was skilfully descriptive and creative, often with a visual dimension.

Tight drainpipe trousers were 'pull family trousers' because the whole family had to help the wearer to put them on. Men who dressed in flashy colours were called 'city boys'. Both were usually regarded as non-traditional and somewhat foolish.

Tight skirts were 'cross no gutter skirts', because those who wore them had difficulty in crossing the open gutters that drain many Nigerian cities.

'Push me, push you' was a locally brewed drink made from banana skins. It was a potent drink and did, indeed, cause a lot of aggression.

Styles of haircuts had colourful names including a 'President Kennedy cut'.

The 'come-back tomorrow' was, of course, bureaucracy.

* * *

Village people treated new ideas, particularly from strangers, with suspicion. They had more trust in their own common sense and they were often right! In the parish hall, an American agriculturist was promoting the use of fertilisers to a group of farmers. After the customary speeches of welcome, the visitor began in a distinctive American accent:

'Folks, I want to talk to you about improving your farming methods. The fertiliser in these bags can help you get a greater crop yield. It works very simply. If you spread it on your fields you get three crops every year. Is that clear? Does anybody want to ask a question?'

There was a deadly silence. Some farmers looked in amazement, others stared in disbelief. The visitor tried again: 'Any questions?'

After a few moments one old man responded:

'Yes sir, would you please repeat what you said, we don't understand.'

This time, the American spoke slowly.

There was another silence. Some of the farmers lowered their heads and looked at the ground. A few rubbed their faces and scratched their heads. Eventually, much to the relief of the visitor, one old farmer stood up, removed the chewing stick from his mouth, took off his tattered hat and adjusted his trousers that were slipping from his hips.

'Thank you, sir. But did I hear you properly? You said if we use this stuff in those bags we will get three crops every year.'

The visitor smiled: 'Yes, man. I guess you got it right.'

Then the old man turned to his fellow farmers with a shrewd look: 'Aha, that's fine. So if we use this stuff, we'll only have to farm every third year.'

The farmers had no intention of changing, risking crop failure by using a product which, for them, was untried. For a people who depended solely on their produce for survival, crop failure would mean starvation and death. Their visitor would be comfortably home in America long before the results of any such experiment were known.

In the same hall, a group of village women listened to a visiting health worker teaching preventative medicine and community hygiene. To illustrate her lesson, the visitor used a chart with a large fly drawn on it:

'My dear friends, it is important for all of us to know how to keep ourselves and our families healthy. Food that's bad can make us sick. Flies like this can carry disease and contaminate food when they land on it. So, it's important to keep food covered to prevent flies landing on it. Do you understand?'

The women seemed to be distracted by the chart and looked at it in wonderment. The visitor repeated what she said using very simple language.

'Would anybody like to comment on what I have said?'

No one answered. Some of the women looked at each other and seemed puzzled. Eventually one robust woman stood up and said quite firmly:

'Thank you, miss, for telling us about those flies. I understand what you said. They could make our food bad and if we eat bad food we can become sick. However, there's something I must tell you. You're a stranger here and may not understand that we don't have those kind of flies in our country. Flies here are much smaller than that.'

* * *

Fund-raising was part of the social life of the communities. One of the most popular forms of fund-raising was the 'bazaar', sometimes called the harvest feast, which was held annually. The Christians of the parish erected stalls made with bamboo poles and palm branches. Food and handcrafts were sold in the stalls by different Christian groups.

It was a great honour to be selected as the chairperson of the bazaar. Mr Stephen Obiora was held in high esteem in the local community and often received that honour. As a successful entrepreneur, with a lucrative road transport business, he was known in the parish as a great motivator of people. Obiora was impressively dressed in a traditional gown – free-flowing, bright-yellow and richly embroidered. Above it, matching soft headgear lay to the left of his head. His ensemble was completed by white long-toed shoes which had multi-coloured plastic decorations.

As the evening light became fainter, the bright lights were switched on around the grounds. Obiora stood erect on a high platform, roofed with palm branches. The crowd had reached almost two thousand and a few wealthy traders had arrived in their prestigious Mercedes. Microphone in hand, Obiora announced the opening of the auction which was one of the main events:

'Ladies and gentlemen, good evening and welcome to the bazaar auction which will open with the sale of a very special and valuable article. Just look at this wonderful matchbox.'

Obiora held it high to the left, centre and then to the right of the crowd:

'You see it's beautifully shaped and has the most attractive colours. It's very special because there are no matches inside but it's full of the wonderful, unpolluted fresh air of Aguleri, the likes of which you can't find in any other part of the world.'

The people roared with laughter and applauded loudly. By this time the attendance had increased greatly, and those in the front rows were pushed against the rope fence that was meant to keep them some distance from the platform.

'Now, who'll make the first bid for this valuable matchbox. C'mon, I need a first bid. Thank you, ladies and gentlemen.'

As Obiora stared at Anthony Ezeani, a wealthy businessman, he scratched his head, grunted and then shouted: '£200.'

Obiora smiled happily and, in a loud, excited voice said:

'Great. Do I hear £200 from Mr Anthony Ezeani?'

Ezeani nodded in agreement.

'Any other bids? Any advance on £200? OK, let's bid,' he said, looking at Ezeani's main business competitor, Maurice Mbanefo.

There was silence, Mbanefo looked at the ground, rubbed

his face, cleared his throat and put his right hand in the air before shouting: 'Yes sir, £500.'

The crowd roared in delight. Women hugged each other and men slapped their right hands together high over their heads. People clapped Mbanefo on the back and congratulated him. Obiora joined in the compliments.

'Thank you, Mr Mbanefo. Fantastic. Well done.'

His voice could hardly be heard with the applause of the crowd.

'Just a minute, my brothers and sisters. We can't let this beautiful, valuable article go for a pittance. Let's have some more bids. OK, let's go. Any more bids? Any advance on £500?'

He looked all around, but there were no bids. Silence fell on the crowd. Then a deep, loud voice was heard from the back row. Obiora could see Amadeus Oguama, MP, with his hand in the air: '£1,500, I bid.'

There was genuine delight among the people. They shouted, clapped and then broke out in chant, as they stamped their feet in dance to the words:

'Oguama, ama, ama, Oguama, ama, ama.'

Obiora tried in vain to restore order, appealing:

'Just a moment, ladies and gentlemen. Mr Amadeus Oguama, MP, has just bid £1,500. Any advance on £1,500?'

'Any advance,' he repeated in the deadly silence that followed.

'OK. Going for £1,500, ... going, ... going, ... gone.'

The people around Oguama hugged him, clapped him forcefully on the back and then lifted him shoulder-high on to the platform to receive the empty matchbox. The crowd started singing as they moved their bodies to the rhythm of the chant: 'Oguama, ama, ama, Oguama, ama, ama.'

Oguama was ecstatically happy, a shrewd politician who had just bought £1,500 worth of prestige and status.

* * *

Recalling those happy days in Aguleri was like looking in a

kaleidoscope. Events, places and people jostled for my attention, rather than coloured beads and stones. Every little thing seemed to tumble them over in my brain-box, creating new, ever more vivid and colourful patterns in my mind.

With a start, I realised it was almost three in the morning. It had been a long day and I would need my wits about me when I reached Rome.

Many chants, all happy ones, closed in on me and lulled me to sleep.

CHAPTER 2

Desperate Smugglers

A gentle waft of coffee brought me fully awake as Skip handed me a mug. 'Sorry to wake you, Tony, but I didn't think you'd want to miss this! Dawn will be in about five minutes and, five minutes later, the Niger should be visible on both sides. I guess you'll be able to see it for ten minutes.'

As Skip returned to the cabin the sun rose, seemingly on cue. Even though I had seen it many times, I could never get over the sense of exuberance that the sudden dawn in the tropics brought. I had never seen it like this, though, high in an aircraft speeding its way north towards the Sahara.

The sun streamed in from the right, lighting the cabin brilliantly, as I stared out to the left, waiting for the first glimpse of the Niger. When it came, I ran from side to side to see as much as I possibly could. It was an amazing sight from the air, a very substantial river, even 1400 miles upstream.

It was easy to remember the river down at Onitsha, with its constant traffic bustling across the mile-and-a-half journey to Asaba and the great suspension bridge, so recently built, that had been an early casualty of the war.

As the river slid gently down the aircraft wing, my mind drifted back to those happy, peaceful days travelling by canoe to the bush schools and villages near its banks, and those of the Anambra. That peaceful life I shared with the Igbo people had its roots in a culture that promoted an orderly society, a culture that had seemed as secure and as tranquil as the river itself. My view of the Niger was finally cut off by the advancing wing-tip.

It was gone.

* * *

Over a period of five years, normal life in Nigeria had been disrupted by a succession of bloody coups d'état. The most violent of these was the 1967 revolution which resulted in the establishment of Biafra, with its own government, currency and national anthem.

The Biafran people were mainly from the Igbo tribe, a people who had been keenly enthusiastic about progress and development. Their education had made them the administrators throughout the new Nigeria. This was soon resented, leading to ugly scenes where Igbos were beaten and killed as they were driven back to their own small homeland in the south-east. Their leaders believed that they could no longer continue as part of Nigeria, and seceded. Biafra did not enjoy full international recognition. Nigeria declared war on 6 July 1967, pitting 34 million Nigerians against 14 million Biafrans in a cruel and bitter struggle that would continue until January 1970.

In an effort to force a surrender, Nigeria set up a total blockade by land, sea and air. This blockade made life extremely difficult, causing great scarcities of essential commodities, especially medicines and protein foods.

* * *

Onitsha was the principal crossing point between East and West Nigeria, an important trading centre on the banks of the Niger. A few miles downstream, the great river started to divide into the many outlets which formed its delta – known locally as the Rivers area. The town was one of the largest in Biafra, with a population of around 300,000 people. One-and-a-half times as many more lived in the immediate area.

Francis Arinze was the Archbishop and I was one of a large number of Spiritans (Holy Ghost) priests and brothers from Ireland under his jurisdiction. I was working in the Social Training Centre at Onitsha, my main task being to promote social development and workers' education. Since I was not attached to a parish, I was often asked to tackle the odd jobs, too. The situation created by the blockade grew more and more depressing. It made many of us weep just to look at the children with their lifeless eyes and their bellies swollen by starvation. But they needed more than our tears. The Archbishop was an Igboman, thirty-six years old, low-sized and fit, with a ready smile for all. Very intelligent, with an outstanding Roman and English academic record, he avoided political involvement, showing mature leadership and a passionate concern for his suffering people.

Arinze called me to his residence to brief him on the effects of the blockade. Dressed as usual in a long white cassock with a wide red sash, he tried in vain to cover his feelings as he greeted me with a smile. But the tenseness in his voice revealed his mood: 'Fr Tony, my people are trapped in this blockade, nothing is moving in or out of Biafra. How bad is the relief situation?' I answered him frankly. Stocks of protein foods were fast disappearing from the markets and stores. Kwashiorkor was killing many children. The hospitals were full of sick and wounded. There were not enough beds and many patients were lying on the hospital floors. As a result of an alarming scarcity of basic medicines, the death rate from malaria, too, was increasing.

Arinze reflected in silence for a few moments. He was deeply upset and his face showed a lot of strain: 'God protect us from that awful kwashiorkor. I had thought it was something totally new to this country. It certainly wasn't known in Eziowele, where I grew up. Sister Doctor Lucy O'Brien visited me yesterday and was kind enough to clear up many of my misunderstandings. Apparently, there had been isolated cases here, in the old days, if a young child was weaned too abruptly from the mother's breast. The high incidence, now, is entirely due to the shortage of protein caused by the blockade. That is why we must do anything we possibly can to ease the situation.'

Arinze paused, clearly distraught. I wasn't sure whether I should say anything. After some hesitation, I said: 'Yes, I agree, it's awful to see the puffed eyes and faces, the little muscles wasted away, the horrible rash...'

Arinze interrupted: 'I thought that, too, but Sr Lucy tells me the unseen damage is worse. Imagine that this disease attacks the liver of the smallest children – the liver, for goodness sake – and can damage the brain. That awful, soft red hair is very distressing. The children are obviously in great pain. The crying is heartbreaking for their parents...'

Arinze was silent for several minutes. This time, I waited. 'The situation is indeed desperate but what can we do? We're totally blockaded by land, sea and air. It's impossible to get in or out of Biafra. But we must do whatever we can. If you can do something to help my people, please do so. Always know that you have my support. I trust that you will be prudent. Don't take unnecessary risks.'

I had left the Archbishop's residence wondering what could be done to break through the blockade for food and medicines. Politics could take its course, but the Igbo children couldn't wait. *Something* had to be done. 'Better to light a candle than curse the darkness...'

Some Igbo friends told me that smugglers were operating to Cameroon from villages in the Calabar area. Their main base was Oron and they used small, locally made, boats with outboard engines – ideal for the creeks in the area. My friends advised me to meet Julius, the head of a group of smugglers. He was an experienced man who could get anything in or out and would probably be happy to bring in supplies for me. The only limit was the size of his boat.

I met Julius outside his wooden hut. Home-made boats were tied to tree stumps nearby. When he saw me approaching, he removed his chewing stick from his mouth and stood up from his cane chair to greet me. Courteously, he offered me his chair, then went to his hut and brought out a stool for himself. As we introduced ourselves, three young men joined us. They greeted me warmly and then sat on the ground, beside their leader.

Not much time was wasted with preamble but it was long enough for each of us to study the other, forming those first, vital impressions. Long rubber boots peeped out from under his faded blue cord trousers. His torn green T-shirt was freshly washed. A red baseball cap with a large peak cast a shadow over his wrinkled face. The relaxed dress spoke of a man sure of himself and his surroundings and yet I sensed that he was a little uneasy, probably not used to white visitors. I will never understand why, but I felt instinctively that I could trust this unpretentious, tall man in his forties whose bright brown eyes blinked frequently as we smiled at each other.

'Julius, I've come to ask your assistance. I'd like to transport medical and food supplies from Cameroon to Biafra. I wonder would you help me?'

'It's very dangerous these days, Father. The Nigerian gun boats are giving us a lot of trouble. We travel through the creeks because it's safer that way.'

'That's OK. I need to buy supplies in Cameroon and arrange the evacuation of sick and old missionaries who may want to leave Biafra later on.'

'You're welcome, but our boats aren't comfortable and it's a long journey.'

I nodded: 'Don't worry about that. Let's discuss the cost of a return trip.'

Some tough bargaining with Julius concluded with a mutually acceptable price. Considering the risks involved, I thought he was quite reasonable.

Arriving in Cameroon gave me a great feeling of freedom. It felt like paradise on earth, with no fear of air-raids, bombing or shelling. I stood in amazement looking at the well-fed, healthy people in the local markets, surrounded by large food stocks, in stark contrast to the situation in Biafra.

I travelled many times with Julius. It was a long journey to Cameroon in the little boat – made even longer by the strict necessity of staying in the cover of the creeks, as much as possible. The boat leaked all the time and I soon became as expert as the others at baling the water out with a tin can. The outboard engine cut out regularly. Nobody but Julius ever touched that motor but he never failed to restart it.

These were minor irritations. My main problem was currency. No one was allowed take money out of Biafra and the soldiers searched us regularly. The problem was solved by stuffing a few large notes in tubes of toothpaste! The trick always worked but it ended my detached status. I was involved now, a real smuggler.

The bright, happy atmosphere of Cameroon, during these brief visits, gave me a respite from the dark tragedy of the blockade. The food and medicine crammed into the boat always seemed pitifully little but it, too, was a little chink in the blockade, one that created new hope for many.

Others found more chinks in the blockade. Frs Dermot Doran, Raymond Kennedy and Fintan Kilbride persuaded many of the pilots who flew Biafran military supplies from Lisbon to Port Harcourt to carry food and medicine parcels, as well. Small chinks, indeed, but they were a start.

These priests highlighted the tragic situation to the media. Nobody could appreciate, then, how important that was to be. New satellites were just beginning to beam television messages around the world. For the first time, ordinary people could see, in their own sittingrooms, what was going on and could feel a sense of involvement in the tragedy. Biafra had been unknown to the rest of the world. Suddenly, it became the top news story.

This was a new television era. New communication technology spawned new skills which helped to save a million lives in Biafra. Since then, these phenomenal developments have changed the whole world's perception of war.

* * *

Onitsha was under constant attack and in danger of being captured. The Nigerians were encamped on the west bank of the Niger and were shelling the town in preparation for an invasion across the river. I had just returned from Cameroon and was horrified at what I saw and the speed of its happening.

Travelling by road was extremely hazardous. There was heavy shelling from the big guns across the river and the MiGs seemed to be everywhere, looking for targets to strafe, preferably anything that moved. Throughout the bombardment, Fr Donal O'Sullivan drove constantly from town to town seeking food for the emergency feeding centres.

Late that evening, as it was getting dark, Donal arrived at my house looking weary. The only food I had was some boiled yam and a few sardines but, after a quick shower, even that worked wonders. When he had finished eating and we had exchanged some general news, he asked me to help Martin Okafor's wife, Maureen, and their three young children to get to Cameroon. Martin was the Biafran Government Administrator of the region and had been falsely accused of being a traitor by some sectors of the Biafran army. He would make an ideal scapegoat for their failure to defend Onitsha. The fact that his wife was Irish, a foreigner, might make things worse.

We put the arrangements in place quickly. The main thing I needed was a formal letter from Martin asking the army and other Biafran officials to facilitate the evacuation of his wife and children. Much later that night, Martin telephoned me:

'For God's sake, Tony, help me. Our intelligence unit has just informed me that the Nigerians are about to cross the Niger. Our supplies are very low, so we won't be able to hold Onitsha for long. Feelings are running very high and I'm in danger from my own people. Please help Maureen and the children to evacuate. They're in serious danger, too.'

'OK, Martin, but I need your letter…'

'No trouble. The letter is already done. Annette is the youngest and she's almost five. She's a good little girl, who'll do what Maureen says. She won't be any trouble… I'm really very grateful…'

'We have a saying in Ireland, Martin. "There will be another day".'

'"Beidh lá eile,"' he interrupted, 'isn't that it in your language? Maureen keeps repeating it. She has the children saying it now.'

'And she's right. Don't worry, Martin. My friends and I will get Maureen and the children to Cameroon. I suggest you give her the letter and get them over here at first light tomorrow. If the situation worsens, send them earlier but phone me if you can.'

His voice became very quiet: 'It might be better if I sent them now, Tony.'

'OK, Martin. I'll be ready.'

The implications of what Martin had said had hardly sunk home by the time Maureen and her children arrived. She kept up a brave front but her red-rimmed eyes and those of the children told another story.

The journey to Oron was long and stressful. Because of the major attack, there were many more checkpoints, each of them taking longer than usual. After about a third of the journey, we stopped at yet another barrier. A young soldier told us that we must wait until his colleague returned. We could see an officer speaking to the other soldier nearby. Then the officer strode briskly to his waiting car and left quickly. The older soldier came over to us, told us we could go and turned to the young man: 'Onitsha is taken. The Captain says…'

That was as much as we heard. It was enough. The news was distressing for the Okafars but it also made the soldiers and militia at the check-points even more nervous and excited for some time. At one checkpoint, an army officer recognised Maureen and called her aside. I had a few anxious moments, wondering whether to intervene, before she returned.

'It's all right, Daddy's safe,' she said, smiling and hugging the children in turn. 'That officer is a friend of Martin's, Tony, and he told me that Martin and the others were evacuated safely to Uli. Oh, thank God.'

As soon as we were clear of the checkpoint, she turned to the children again, with a big smile. This time she spoke softly in Irish: 'Beidh lá eile againn, cinnte. Buíochas mór le Dia.'

To my astonishment, the children began chanting and clapping:

'Beidh lá eile againn, beidh lá eile againn.'

As Maureen had said, that other day was sure now, great thanks to God. The journey seemed a lot easier after that and we were soon in Oron, where I introduced a tired but happy Maureen and her children to Julius. He agreed to take them to Cameroon immediately, and at a reasonable price. As we made our way to the boat, heavy rain started to fall and I asked Julius to wait while I tried to get some raincoats. At the local convent, the Holy Child Sisters were most generous, one finding some light raincoats and a travel container of water, while another made fresh sandwiches from their limited food. When I returned to the jetty, I was surprised to find that Julius had left. Raphael, one of his boatmen, met me:

'Julius told me to tell you he couldn't wait any longer. The jetty is very exposed. We heard that some MiGs had been strafing targets not too far away. Julius thought it would be safer in the creeks, so he left quickly.'

'Thanks for telling me but I don't know what to do now. Those children and their mother will need this clothing and food for the journey.'

Raphael made a suggestion: There's a white man at the other jetty. He's leaving for Cameroon, soon. Maybe he could help you.'

I walked to the other jetty and met the white man. When I introduced myself and told him my problem, he didn't hesitate:

'Name's Parker, Padre, British High Commissioner's office. I've chartered a boat and you're welcome to travel to Cameroon with me.'

I had heard much about Parker on Biafran radio broadcasts. He had been stationed in Enugu and was publicly condemned as a spy. Mobs of angry Biafrans had recently demonstrated outside his office, demanding his expulsion, dancing and chanting: 'Pack Parker, pack Parker'. The police had to disperse the demonstrators to avoid serious violence.

Parker had a striking appearance. Clearly a professional diplomat, he was impeccably, if inappropriately, dressed for the journey on the make-shift boat. His soft, non-intrusive voice and kindly smile suggested that he would be an ideal man for politically sensitive situations. I was somewhat reluctant to accept his invitation because travelling with a public enemy of Biafra could make me guilty by association. However, I realised I had no option:

'That's very kind of you, Mr Parker. I appreciate your generous offer.'

'Good, meet Linus my boatman.'

Linus had an outboard engine that was just a little more powerful than the engines on the other boats. As a result, his was the fastest of the smugglers' boats and he was very proud of the fact.

We were soon into the meandering creeks and the only sign of our progress was a gentle rippling of the waters in our wake. Towering, majestic palm trees and general overgrowth flanked us protectively, often joining overhead to shade us from the scorching sun. The air was scented with the freshness of virgin soil. Colourful tropical birds flitted between the treetops, their protests at our intrusion occasionally penetrating the drone of the outboard engine. Here, nature was in charge, seemingly oblivious to the war a few miles away. The creeks widened and narrowed along the way. At one narrow part, we found Julius, stopped.

A withered palm tree had fallen across the narrow part of the creek, resting on its banks. Linus and Julius looked dumbfounded, Maureen almost in tears. Parker gazed at me in silence for a while, both of us trying to mask our emotions. Then he shrugged helplessly, looked a shade paler and seemed to have trouble enunciating his words.

'Er, Padre, another damn blockade. I presume it won't be

possible to pass. We can't stay here and it will be dark soon.
Let's get back to Oron.'

'Wait a little, Mr Parker, let's see what can be done.'

I looked at Linus at the end of the boat. He had opened a
wooden box beside the engine and was removing oily clothes
and a few tools. Then he reached for the bottom of the box,
laughed and shouted: 'Aha, I found it.'

We all wondered what he was talking about. Then he took
a machete out of the box, joyfully beating the air with it and
shouting: 'Hey, Julius, we're OK now. Tie up your boat beside
mine. C'mon, help me cut the tree.'

The two friends walked across the tree until they reached
its narrowest point. Sitting astride it, they took turns chop-
ping it until it broke in two and pushed aside one end until
there was sufficient space for the boats to pass. With great
relief, we congratulated them on their achievement.

As we approached Ikang, the last Biafran outpost, I saw a
number of soldiers lying on the ground some distance from
the water. As they pointed their guns at us, I realised that
Parker was their target. He became nervous and his voice
quivered with frustration: 'They're after me, Padre. What
should I do?'

'Take cover, just lie down and keep quiet!'

I left the boat and walked over to the soldiers. I recognised
Ahaji and Idigo from earlier journeys. They shook hands
with me and seemed genuinely happy to see me again.

'My friends, what's going on?'

John Idigo's face froze: 'We've orders to shoot Parker. He's a
British spy.'

I pleaded with these young, inexperienced soldiers:

'Hold on, my friends, do you know what you're doing? If
you shoot this man, you'll make people overseas believe that
Biafrans are bad people. If that happens, no one will support
Biafra. If you really want Biafra to survive, you must prove to
the world that you're not murderers.'

Nick Ahaji stared at me with an officious expression:

'We have our orders.'

'I know you have, but who told you to shoot Parker?'

'Captain Okoye in Calabar,' they answered together.

'But he's not in charge of Biafra. I'm sure Colonel Ojukwu would not want Parker shot. Okoye is only a small man and maybe he was drunk when he gave you the order to shoot. I suppose he likes to booze.'

'Yes, he does. He's often drunk.'

'OK, I think it would be good to let Parker go. After all, if he leaves the country he can't spy on Biafra again.'

The soldiers nodded to each other in agreement. Ahaji waved his right hand. 'Right, we'll let him go but I hope we don't get into trouble for it.'

I gathered my kit to leave the boat and told Linus: 'Go as fast as you can and don't stop until you arrive in Cameroon.'

Parker made an effort to smile: 'Padre, I'll never forget what you've done.' It was a short walk to Julius' boat to give Maureen the clothing and food. Handshakes were exchanged all round as I entrusted her and the children to Julius for the rest of the journey to Cameroon.

When the two boats had left, I suddenly realised that it was getting late and I had no place to stay for the night. I turned to Ahaji: 'Is there a mission near here? I need somewhere to sleep tonight.'

'Yes, about twelve miles down that road, there's a maternity hospital in Ikot Ene where some Sisters work. You should try there.'

It was getting late in the evening and the light was fading gently. I walked on the laterite road through small villages where children called their friends to see the strange white man. Some presumed I was a priest and waved at me. Others kept quiet, doubtful. Priests usually travelled by car in that area. As the dusk was darkening into night, I tried to walk faster, hoping to arrive in Ikot Ene before it was totally dark. The weight of the holdall bag with a change of clothes and shaving gear slowed me down. I became desperately thirsty as perspiration clamped my shirt to my body.

I arrived at the hospital very dishevelled, not having washed or shaved for two days. The Sisters, who hadn't met me previously, were suspicious and thought I might be a mercenary. To add to their distrust, I foolishly told them the story of Parker. Sr Mary, the Superior, had a cadaverous face hollowed by the fatigue of overwork and too many night calls. A woman in her early forties, she looked at me dumb-founded, wondering how to handle this strange visitor.

'Have a cup of tea and then we'll see what we can do to find you a bed for the night. I hope you'll understand that we have a lot of work to do and it's not easy for us to look after visitors.'

Tea was served in the parlour while the Sisters discussed behind doors what they would do with this suspicious-looking man who said he was a priest. Mary returned to the parlour: 'Sorry we can't give you a bed in the convent but you're welcome to stay in one of the small empty wards in the hospital. When you've finished your tea, I'll show you your bed.'

I quickly drank the tea and followed her.

'There you are now, sleep well. The shower's at the end of the ward.'

I looked at the maternity bed with its baby cot attached and smirked: 'Sister, I hope nobody will be disappointed if there isn't a delivery for this admission.'

Mary bade me goodnight, without a smile, and left the ward. I had a cold shower that was most refreshing and slept soundly. My deep sleep was interrupted at about six o'clock next morning by voices outside the ward. I recognised Ahaji's:

'Where's Byrne, the priest who came here last night? Come on, show us where he is. Quick, do you hear me? Bring me to him now.'

The nurse tried to stand up to him: 'You must report to the

matron. You can't come into a maternity hospital like this and disturb everyone.'

'Shut up, who do you think you are, you foolish woman? Did you hear what I said? Bring me to Byrne or I'll beat you up.'

I lay still on the bed. A thin stream of sweat moved down my spine as the terrified nurse showed Ahaji to the ward.

As Ahaji pushed open the doors, the others rushed in and pointed their AK 47s at me. Their new combat uniforms, camouflage helmets and shining black boots seemed altogether more menacing in these surroundings.

Ahaji cleared his throat and screeched:

'Byrne, you're under arrest. We've received a radio message from our commanding officer to take you to Calabar prison. Get dressed and come with us immediately.'

I said nothing for a few minutes but blinked. It all seemed so unreal, like a bad dream, but it wasn't. This was real. The soldiers were like excited boy scouts on their first camp outing, clearly enjoying their role in arresting a collaborator of a British spy, an enemy of Biafra.

I had decided to put a brave face on the situation when the funny part of it struck me. This could be history in the making – the first priest to be arrested in a maternity hospital, lying in a bed with a baby's cot attached.

'Welcome, my friends, I know you have to take me to Calabar. That's no problem but you'll understand that I have to wash, shave and celebrate Mass. After that we can have breakfast together and make our way to Calabar.'

Ahaji spoke for them: 'OK, but don't delay too long.'

'That's good. Now, tell me why I am being placed under arrest?'

Ahaji's eyes flickered and he hesitated before giving a frank, candid reply: 'You helped a British spy to escape. We should have shot him but you convinced us not to. You'll be charged with helping one of our enemies.'

I shuddered involuntarily, completely stunned at the

thought of that serious charge. In time of war that could mean death. Somehow, I had assumed that any charge would be an administrative one – showing disrespect to an officer, perhaps. The more senior officers were probably glad to be shut of Parker, avoiding the problems of a trial.

My immediate worry was my passport. There were Nigerian immigration stamps on it which could be enough to condemn me as a spy. I could be shot. Put it in the cistern of the toilet or keep it? It was a big decision. I dithered for a while, finally deciding to keep it and chance the consequences.

The soldiers were reverent during Mass but I would have chosen a different congregation in that convent chapel. It could be my last Mass before the firing squad! Afterwards, Sr Mary brought us to the small refectory in the convent. Despite the scarcities, we were served porridge, milk, bread, jam and tea. 'Sorry, we've no sugar. It's impossible to find anywhere.'

I forced myself to eat, knowing that my next meal was uncertain. I felt sorry for the Sisters, though. Food was scarce and the healthy appetites of the soldiers must have made large inroads into their meagre stocks.

Ahaji became less formal and more personal during breakfast. His voice became quite friendly: 'Hi, it's a long time since I was at Mass. I used to be an altar boy at Uturu when I was at school there.'

I tried to maintain this cordiality: 'What school did you go to, Ahaji?' His mouth softened as he smiled: 'The Marist Brothers. They were my friends, especially Br Frank. He was tough, made us work hard, but he really liked sports and games and, as a result, we all liked them, too.'

As soon as breakfast was finished, the soldiers escorted me to a camouflaged Landrover. I was sandwiched between two young soldiers who pointed their guns at my side. As we travelled at breakneck speed on the bumpy road to Calabar, I prayed that the safety-catches of the guns were secure.

At the prison, a security officer brought me into a dark room with a small window secured by strong iron bars. A large bulb hung from the ceiling over a dusty table on which a tattered old psychology magazine lay. Ahaji guarded me anxiously, with his AK 47 cocked to impress the security officer. After some time a tall middle-aged man entered the room. He had a bushy beard, with dark glasses slipping uncomfortably down his nose. Traditional marks engraved on his forehead and pointed filed teeth clearly identified him with his clan. His faked American accent highlighted his limited English as he placed a cardboard file on the table. It was marked in large grey lettering: 'Government of Biafra, Intelligence Unit, Strictly Confidential.'

He removed a few large sheets of lined paper from the file, placed them on the desk and took a pen from his pocket. His eyes were riveted on me and his look was angry as he scowled: 'Your name?'

'Tony Byrne.'

'Your full name.'

'Anthony Michael Patrick Byrne.'

He took a long time to write that down, making me sorry that I hadn't thought of many more. He looked at me again, as he carefully adjusted the glasses which had been slipping from his nose. 'Your father's name?'

As he wrote that down, he adjusted the glasses again. It was obviously a long-standing ritual and I enjoyed the thought that the glasses were winning! 'Your mother's name?'

When he had noted the names and many other details, he asked for my passport. I gave it to him and watched him, anxiously thinking of the Nigerian stamps. He tried to read the introduction which was in Irish. Switching to the English translation, he was still reading very slowly. To pass the time, I tried to remember the archaic wording:

We, Minister for External Affairs of Ireland, hereby request and require all those whom it may concern to allow the bearer, a citizen

of Ireland, to pass freely without let or hindrance and to afford
the bearer all necessary assistance and protection.

That request from the Irish Foreign Minister didn't seem to
make any impression on him. He read five or six more pages
and seemed exhausted before he reached the visa pages
where the Nigerian stamps were. Then he wrote a few lines
before turning arrogantly to Ahaji: 'Soldier, take the prisoner
away until we arrange further investigations.'

Ahaji led me off to a cell. On the way, I asked one of the
warders to get me the commanding officer. He told me that
'the Major' was too busy to see me. I started shouting, hoping
that some of the Christian prison officers might do something
to help me. My throat became quite sore as the officers argued
among themselves but, eventually, the commanding officer
came to see me. He was a small man, dressed in a smart new
uniform decorated with silver stars and gold braid. Heart
pounding, blood hammering in my ears, I searched for suitable words to appeal for my release. Then I glanced briefly at
the commanding officer's face as he stood beside the three
prison warders.

He looked a little familiar but...

I blinked to clear my eyes, straining to study his face. I was
looking at an old friend, Emmanuel Okpara from Aguleri. I
remembered him as the former head boy in a local school. He
had later studied in a military college and been a major in the
Nigerian army before defecting to the Biafran side.

He looked very embarrassed:

'Hey, my good friend, Father Tony. How are you? I'm
sorry all this has happened. You must forgive these young
soldiers. They've no experience. I didn't know you were the
one they arrested. Relax for a few moments and I'll arrange
transport for you to the nearby mission.'

'Thanks, Emmanuel. I'd appreciate that. Please ask the
security officer who interrogated me to return my passport.'

He ordered one of his assistants to get the passport, and I
was driven to the local mission in an army jeep, astonished at

the simplicity of my release, but relieved and happy to be free again – until the next time!

The bishops in Nigeria and Biafra made tireless efforts to promote peace but the blockade made communications difficult. On a number of occasions, I acted as the courier carrying proposals between the bishops. Julius brought me to Cameroon. From there, I took a regular flight to Lagos.

The Biafran stamps on my passport were almost as dangerous in Lagos as the Nigerian stamps were in Biafra. Going through Lagos Airport with the incriminating stamps became a nerve-racking experience.

I built up a series of questions and comments to distract the officers who stamped my passport. The simpler they were, the better they worked. My favourite was a flamboyant invitation to 'come and visit my country, Ireland'. Distracting the officers was useful, but I often felt that distracting myself from the risks involved was more important!

These trips to Nigeria made me one of the very few people who could see at first hand what was happening to people's feelings in both Nigeria and Biafra.

Nigerians identified Biafra with the Igbo tribe. The vast majority of Biafrans were Igbo people and the Nigerians believed that the Igbos had instigated the revolution that led to the establishment of the breakaway state.

During one of my visits to Lagos, I saw Nigerian soldiers and civilians rounding up Igbo people and whipping them in public. It was most disturbing but worse still was the sight of the bodies of dead Igbos on the streets the next day. Later on, a law was passed in Nigeria that all Igbos must be registered, causing them to fear that they might be rounded up and killed.

In Biafra, a high proportion of the people were well educated. The militia, however, was a vigilante organisation that had many young men and women with little or no formal education. This militia often harassed civilians, set up unnecessary road blocks and generally was a law unto itself. Its members were armed and sometimes irresponsible.

The militia and their checkpoints made life incredibly difficult. Some militia insisted on inspecting our watches, in case they had James Bond-style devices in them. Others confused the words missionaries with mercenaries but the most difficult explanation I had to make was why my Irish passport had a harp on it. The fact that Guinness use the harp as a logo, and had a brewery in Lagos, made me a suspicious character, again! Silly things can take on another dimension when there are guns involved!

As I was leaving Julius' boat one day, some militia surrounded me. One of them shouted: 'Hey, this fellow looks like a British spy, let's deal with him.' He continued quietly: 'I think he's trying to fool us, pretending to be a missionary. He's wearing what they wear but he's not a missionary.'

The others stared at me and agreed that I was a fake, using the missionary dress as a camouflage. Missionaries dressed in long white cassocks with a black cincture, or cord, around the waist and reaching to the ankles. One of them grabbed me by this cincture. He started chanting and the others joined in: 'British spy, British spy.'

Some local people rushed over to see what was going on. I felt I was in serious trouble. The crowd increased and the excitement mounted. They walked me through a market place where women sold foodstuffs. One woman rushed over to me. Her face showed determination. Standing in front of the militia with her hands outstretched to stop them, she shouted:

'What are you boys doing? Listen to me, stop this! You're doing a bad thing. God will punish you, I'm warning you. This man is a priest. I saw him saying Mass in our parish some time ago. Stop this nonsense. He's not a British spy. He's one of our Reverend Fathers.'

One of the militia approached her threateningly: 'Mama, stand out of the way or I'll beat you. Stand back.'

The woman was more determined than ever: 'My son, you

can beat me if you like but I'm not moving. Why don't you bring this priest to the barracks and the soldiers there will deal with the case.'

The militia looked at each other. Eventually one said: 'OK, Mama, we will.'

They paraded me to the barracks. 'Mama' came with me and I felt secure when she was by my side. When we arrived at the barracks, the militia asked for Captain Ejiofor. After some time he came along.

'Now, what's all this about? What's the palaver?'

One of the militia saluted Ejiofor: 'Sir, we caught this man coming from Cameroon on a boat. He's a British spy and we want him arrested.'

'Mama' interrupted: 'Hey, this is nonsense. He's one of our priests. I saw him saying Mass in our parish a few weeks ago. Officer, these boys are talking nonsense, you must stop them acting like this.'

Ejiofor asked me a few questions about my identity and said: 'I'll send some of my men with you to the local Catholic mission for identification.'

He turned to the militia: 'You can go there with him. If the priests at the mission can identify him as a priest, we'll know he's not a British spy.'

The Society of St Patrick's Missionaries (Kiltegans) worked here. Most of these priests wouldn't know me because I had never worked in the area. A catechist met us when we arrived at the mission house. The militia asked him to call the priest in charge. When the priest came out, I stared at him in amazement. It was Des Perry, a classmate of mine at St Vincent's, in Dublin. He was the only one in my class that I didn't like. I had been somewhat jealous of him because he came from a well-to-do business family but now I was so excited to see him that I shouted: 'Perry. Des Perry! How are you? This is Tony Byrne, your old school-mate. God, I'm glad to see you.'

'For heaven's sake, Byrne, I don't believe it. What's going on? You haven't changed much.'

He gave me a warm embrace: 'It's great to see you, Byrne.'

The militia were quiet. The one who held my cincture let it slip as the others lowered their heads in embarrassment.

'Mama' was very happy and shouted at them: 'You foolish boys. I told you that he was a priest and you wouldn't listen. You made this priest suffer so much, you should be punished for this.' Then she turned to me: 'Sorry that these boys treated you like this, Father. They're stupid people and I will tell my people that they should control their sons. Please rest now with Father Perry.'

I thanked her for what she had done. She said she would come to visit me later on to see that I was alright.

Des was very hospitable. We laughed and joked about old times. Then I added reflectively: 'It's strange, isn't it, Des, to think that I didn't like you in school and now you've saved my skin.'

He laughed loudly: 'I hope I won't live to regret it.'

* * *

As I thought about the early days in Biafra, I was surprised that I seemed to remember every detail about the food on each occasion ... Sister Mary who had no sugar, and apologised ... The kindness of the Holy Child Sisters in Oron raiding their depleted larder to make sandwiches ... My exhausted Superior, Father Donal, relishing a few slices of boiled yam and sardines ... In normal times, most people are proud of their hospitality but, in times like these, when the next supply of food is uncertain, hospitality requires a certain foolhardiness or heroism – or faith. Perhaps it takes a mixture of all three.

Henry's voice, from the public address system, broke in to my musings: 'Tony, I hope you're hanging in there. We're just coming up to half-way. I'll drop down for a chat with you later.'

CHAPTER 3

The Gunrunner's Cargo

Half way. Suddenly, I felt annoyed at myself, furious even, that I had wasted half of this precious interlude in a reverie. In a few hours we would be in Lisbon and from there I would take an Alitalia flight to Rome.

There might be little time for thinking after we reached Lisbon, and I felt ill-prepared for these vital meetings in the Vatican. What could I say that would persuade diplomats to set aside diplomacy? To a diplomat, what I was proposing might seem close to insanity …

When all else fails, begin at the beginning! There were so many beginnings, though. Perhaps, if the officials were reminded of how the Vatican became involved in the conflict, it might help.

As I wrestled with the problem, I jotted down a few ideas and it all came back to me, in surprising detail. From the beginning, the Vatican, and the Pope himself, had played a crucial part in the relief efforts.

* * *

Asaba town was agog with excitement that day. The streets were lined with schoolgirls and boys from St Bridget's Grammar School and St Patrick's College. Their colourful uniforms gave a pattern to the otherwise riotous profusion of styles, colours and materials worn by the crowds. Their teachers, Marianists and Sisters of Our Lady of the Apostles, were torn between fussing over their charges and joining the large numbers of adults.

Local dignitaries mixed with a group of priests and religious.

Beside them, Archbishop Charles Heerey, of Onitsha, chatted with Bishop Patrick Kelly as they reviewed the scene. Much of newly independent Nigeria was keen to make a good impression on Cardinal Montini, a confidant of the universally popular Pope John XXIII.

Montini's visit would be almost as good as the Pope coming. Christians were very excited. Many non-Christians, too, welcomed the opportunity to show their country to the close representative of a world leader.

Archbishops Montini and Roncalli had both been Vatican diplomats, then neighbouring archbishops in Milan and Venice. On Roncalli's election as Pope John XXIII, Montini had been one of his first choices as cardinal. This time, Montini accepted, having previously declined the honour.

Musicians and dancers held last-minute rehearsals or broke into song and dance anyhow, from sheer exuberance. There were palms everywhere, even some bunting, and the new nation's flag flew proudly on many buildings. When the cardinal's motorcade arrived, the excitement reached fever pitch. The scene which met the cardinal's eyes was a glorious feast of colour and excitement but the most dazzling colours of all sparkled in the eyes of children and adults alike – eyes that twinkled in a sea of laughing, happy faces.

Speeches of welcome jostled with song and dance in a delightful potpourri of sound and colour that combined the traditional and modern, civil and religious, local and international courtesies. The exuberance was infectious. Montini, a shy and modest man, was clearly overwhelmed but graciously accepted the honours offered to him as a distinguished visiting Chief from Rome, a Prince of the Church.

After a little while, Archbishop Heerey led the cardinal to the boat which would carry him the mile and a half across the Niger. Brightly painted in red and blue, the boat was richly decorated with palm branches and bunting. Cut flowers bedecked the cabin and the awning on the deck. A decorated, carved chair with a red cushion stood alone in the centre of that deck.

As the boat moved off, seventeen canoes approached it, each with its complement of richly decorated warriors and musicians, chanting in unison as they paddled to take up their positions as escorts. On a signal, the canoes split into two groups, the seven with the Midwestern markings taking guard on the right, while their ten Igbo colleagues took the left side.

The flotilla moved at a sedate speed, observing all the traditional river courtesies. The warriors alternated between songs of welcome to the visiting Chief and traditional boat songs, Igbo and Midwestern, all accompanied by their musicians with drums, tambourines and the trumpeting of horns made from elephant tusks.

It was an extraordinary sight as the flotilla crossed the lordly Niger in state – one that Cardinal Montini would never forget.

* * *

Just a year after his visit to Nigeria, Cardinal Montini was elected Pope, choosing the name Paul VI. Now, another four years on, these same men who had shown him their skills, honoured him and shared these ceremonial duties in friendship, were at war with each other. It was unthinkable. The Pope's distress increased as reports from church relief workers in Biafra indicated that two thousand children were dying every day. Oxfam put the figure even higher, at three thousand.

Pope Paul was determined that no effort should be spared to try to make peace. He appointed two Papal Peace Delegates, whom he commissioned to visit Nigeria and Biafra in his name. Monsignor Dominic Conway, Rector of the Irish College in Rome, who later became Bishop of Elphin Diocese in Ireland, and Monsignor Georg Rochcau, a Frenchman of Russian extraction working in Secours Catholique, Paris, were his chosen delegates.

When they visited Nigeria on 23 December 1967, they were received with warm hospitality and cordial respect by

General Yakubu Gowon. He was thirty-two years of age, son of a Protestant minister, and came from one of the smallest tribes in the North, the Sho Sho.

Yakubu Gowon had a mission school training. At nineteen, he joined the army and was sent to Eaton Hall – later to Sandhurst, Hythe and Warminster. He became the first Nigerian Adjutant. Low-sized and handsome, always well groomed, he had a dazzling, boyish smile. Many people believed that he was the internationally accepted front-man, courteous with visiting journalists, charming with diplomats and endearing on television.

During a one-hour meeting with Gowon, the peace delegates outlined their mission to Nigeria. They said that they came to preach peace on behalf of the Pope and to give practical expression of his concern for all suffering people, irrespective of their faith or origin.

During the interview with the delegates, Gowon expressed his appreciation of the Pope's interest in the people of Nigeria and assured the delegates of both freedom of passage and safe transit in areas under the control of his forces. He furthermore declared that he was favourable to the delegates' intention of visiting Biafra provided that security could be assured. Unfortunately, he was not in a position to offer that assurance.

Before leaving Nigeria, Conway and Rochcau visited religious authorities of the Catholic, Muslim and Protestant faiths and also the representatives of the International and Nigerian Red Cross.

The delegates found it impossible to visit Biafra because of the blockade and the heavy fighting. Consequently the Government and people of Biafra saw the visit of the Papal Peace Delegates to Nigeria as one-sided. The Bishops of Biafra were called to the State House by the Biafran government to receive an official protest about the unbalanced peace negotiations. Alongside this official protest, there was a public denunciation of the peace negotiations. Many Catholics felt utterly disappointed with their church. Strong anti-Catholic propaganda programmes were broadcast on Biafran radio, causing negative feelings towards the church. The bishops had an emergency meeting to discuss what could be done to address the mounting criticism. They decided to write a letter to the Pope requesting him to send the peace delegates to Biafra via Lisbon.

Early on Christmas Eve 1967, I arrived in St Joseph's parish. Weeks before, Fr Fred Lynch, the local parish priest, had invited me to celebrate three Christmas Masses in outlying villages. We had scarcely time to greet each other before a messenger on a motor-bike arrived with a note marked 'Urgent' and addressed to me.

When I read it, I was dumbfounded. Fred could see the shock in my face and looked quizzically at me but asked no questions. I read the note a second time, then handed it to him

'Read it, I don't know what's going on, Fred.'

He read it aloud, slowly:

'Please leave St Joseph's immediately. Cancel your Christmas Masses. Come here to Dunokofia. It's a matter of grave urgency. Please don't delay. Archbishop Arinze.'

Fred looked anxious:

'Tony, you'd better move fast. It must be really urgent. Arinze would never let any priest cancel Christmas Masses unless there was a very good reason. I'll send a runner to the villages to tell the people. They'll be bitterly disappointed, but there's nothing we can do.'

I was on the road in less than ten minutes, bag packed, and travelling as fast as I could to Dunokofia. As I drove, I tried in vain to guess what had made the Archbishop write such an extraordinary note.

When I arrived at Dunokofia, there were more than twenty thousand displaced people from Onitsha and the neighbour-ing villages standing outside the local school and church, or sitting on the ground under palm trees. They had evacuated their homes as they fled from the shells of the advancing Nigerian army, carrying small bundles of their most treasured possessions.

Church relief workers gave them a daily ration and cooked food to keep them alive. They looked thin and fearful, but relieved to have survived. As they told the stories of how they escaped, they wept. Every now and again, one of the elders would clap his hands and call for silence: 'Shush. A moment please. Listen now everyone.'

Silence would fall on the crowd as people strained to listen to the din of exploding shells in the distance. That sound became louder each time they listened. Everyone feared the day when the din would be so loud that it would signal the start of yet another long march to safety.

Shortly after I arrived at Dunokofia, a man approached me. I recognised Francis at a glance, a church worker I had known in Aguleri a couple of years previously. His friends had constantly teased him about his babyface looks. They wouldn't now, I thought grimly, seeing the strain on his face. He called me aside: 'I don't know whether you heard that your friend Joseph Okafor was killed yesterday. A strafing MiG... Oh, I'm so sorry...'

Not Joseph. It couldn't be. Joseph, who had taught me so much as we travelled around Aguleri... he couldn't be dead. Suddenly, the war seemed much more personal. I turned back to Francis to thank him for telling me and ask for details, but he was already gone. With a start, I remembered that Arinze was waiting for me. Personal grief would have to wait.

Shortly before the town fell, Arinze had left his house in Onitsha, moving with his people to Dunokofia. When I met him in the parish office I could see that the strain of the war was beginning to tell. He was tense, wore a frown that hinted of desperation and he blinked nervously as he greeted me. He cleared his throat before he spoke:

'Sorry about the Christmas Masses. I hope you'll understand. Food and medicines are extremely scarce, the death rate increasing... I don't have to tell you that the country is facing tragedy. The Government and people of Biafra are angry with the church because the Papal Peace Delegates didn't visit us. My fellow bishops and I have decided to make an appeal to the Pope asking him to send the delegates to Biafra through Lisbon. The bishops would like you to take that letter to Rome.'

I was taken aback by this. I knew very little about Rome and absolutely nothing about the workings of the Vatican.

'I'll do all I can to help, Archbishop, but it'll take some time to travel *via* Cameroon to Rome.'

'Because of the urgency, the bishops have requested Colonel Ojukwu to provide transport for you on one of the empty ammunition planes flying to Lisbon. He has agreed. Please go to Port Harcourt immediately and contact an American man there who flies ammunition to Biafra. I don't know his name but everybody knows him at the airport. He'll arrange a flight to Lisbon for you and then you can get a regular flight from there to Rome.'

Security at Port Harcourt Airport on 26 December 1967 was tight. Armed soldiers were everywhere. I spoke to a soldier at the main entrance: 'I'm looking for an American who works for the government. Can you help me?' The soldier looked at me suspiciously: 'Look, we don't have any Americans working for the government. Why do you ask? Write your name and address down and I'll ask my boss if he knows of any American working around here.'

After ten minutes, he returned: 'The head of security wants to see you.' He brought me to an office marked 'strictly no admission'. A middle-aged man sat at a desk laden with cardboard files. 'You say your name is Fr Tony Byrne. Do you have identification papers?'

'Yes. Here's my passport.'

He fingered through it.

'Right, we've just received instructions from our head office that we should provide you with transport to Lisbon. I'll introduce you to Butch Dutting, the American who flies supplies for us. Follow me.'

I followed him through the departure lounge on to the runway where many wooden crates of ammunition were being unloaded from an aircraft. Soldiers' faces appeared from dug-outs where anti-aircraft guns were positioned. A few tanks and a fire engine stood near the runway.

As we approached the plane, a man strode briskly to meet us. The security man introduced him:

'This is Mr Butch Dutting who will fly you to Lisbon.'

'Hi, it's a pleasure to meet you.'

I looked at him in amazement. I had imagined a gunrunner would be rough and, probably, bearded. Instead I met a polite, clean shaven, neatly dressed gentleman in his middle years who had a soft voice and an attractive personality. He was one of the many gunrunners to Biafra who had the confidence of Biafran government officials. In a gentle voice, he said:

'We'll be ready to take-off for Fernando Po in about two hours. We'll gas up there, then fly on to Lisbon. Please wait in the departure lounge.'

After three hours Dutting came to me: 'Sorry, it's not my day. We had to iron out some technical problems. We're ready to go now.'

As we walked to his plane – a propeller-driven Super-constellation – he was apologetic: 'I'm afraid the aircraft is not the best, Tony. The Nigerians nailed us last night and did some damage. Don't be scared, we'll make it to Lisbon all right and I can get the repairs done there.'

I looked fearfully at the old-fashioned, damaged plane, one window covered with plastic sheeting, the fuselage pock-marked from shrapnel. I wondered, frankly, how far we'd get in this dilapidated aircraft. Yet, somehow, Dutting inspired me with confidence. I'd only just met him but I felt sure he wouldn't fly unless the plane was airworthy.

He introduced me casually to his co-pilot and engineer and we were soon airborne. In less than an hour, we landed at Fernando Po, where we refuelled. When we landed, Spanish security officers came on board. They seemed surprised at my presence and asked if I had a visa for Fernando Po.

'I've come from Biafra. There is no Spanish Embassy there.'

'Let me see your passport. No one is allowed to enter here without a visa. Please remain on board until I return.'

He and Dutting left the aircraft. Eventually, Dutting returned:

'It's OK, Tony, you can stay at the departure lounge while we refuel and go through all the formalities for take-off. I guess it would be wise for you not to ask any awkward questions in the departure lounge or take photographs. Let's go and have something to eat.'

We had a light snack together. Dutting seemed totally relaxed, leisurely ordering refills of coffee as we chatted. I had to remind myself that this chap really was a gunrunner. I was puzzled that the crew didn't join us but felt it inappropriate to comment. Perhaps that's the way a Captain works. It was nearly another hour before the co-pilot appeared. Without entering the restaurant, he gave Dutting a thumbs-up sign and Dutting waved in reply before turning to me: 'OK, Tony, we're off.'

'You're a hard taskmaster, Butch. Don't the lads even get a coffee?'

'Oh, didn't I tell you, Tony, they're not coming to Lisbon with us. I don't officially need a crew to ferry a freighter for repairs or to give a friend a lift in the process. They're due a break and they fancied taking it in Fernando Po.'

That left me speechless but, by the time we reached the plane, I had recovered enough to shake hands with the crew and wish them a pleasant holiday before I went on board. It was several minutes before Dutting followed me and invited me to fly with him in the cockpit.

This was a new experience. The cockpit controls fascinated me. Every inch of the dashboard seemed to be covered with dials, instruments and switches. Once we were clear of Fernando Po, I asked Dutting to explain the basics to me. He was delighted. With an enthusiasm that was infectious, he explained the functions of the instruments and many of their idiosyncrasies, as well. I marvelled at the sophisticated simplicity of the joystick and the way its every movement was reflected in the appropriate dials. It seemed that when a dial gave a faulty reading, there was always another which could warn the experienced pilot. Except the altimeter.

With a twinkle in his eye, he said: 'If that goes, you gotta keep an eye out the window. It's no good running into mountains that you think are thousands of feet below you.'

Most of the faults came about as a result of near misses from ack-ack shells. That was part of the price of flying in a war zone, anywhere. The concussion from a big shell exploding, even fifty metres from the aircraft, could damage any instrument on board. The damage mightn't show itself for weeks but the short flight to Fernando Po was normally enough to show up anything serious.

The time passed quickly. Knowing nothing of flying, I plied him with questions. The more searching they were, the more he seemed to enjoy them. Dutting himself intrigued me. It struck me that he was quite like Julius – the same ruthless opportunism coupled with the affectionate handling of his machine. After the talk of damage, I found that curiously reassuring!

At one point, a crisp message came over the radio:

'Mauritania, Mauritania calling. Identify yourself. Over.'

Butch busied himself with his flightplan, explaining that he hadn't sought permission to overfly these countries, but that their signals helped him plot a more accurate course.

'Mauritania, Mauritania calling. Identify yourself. Over.'

Butch winked at me: 'Can't read you clearly. Please repeat. Over.'

'Mauritania, Mauritania calling. Identify yourself. Over.'

When he was happy with his position, he called:

'I regret that... faulty radio... cannot communicate... Over and out.'

Later, I asked him about the threat of Nigerian fighters.

'The greatest risk is close to Biafra. If we flew direct to Lisbon, we would be in easy range for nearly 500 miles and they wouldn't hesitate to shoot us down. In practice, using Fernando Po, we're safe sixty or seventy miles from Port Harcourt. Even if they were sure of our identity, the Nigerians would be unsure, diplomatically, about attacking a 'totally innocent flight' between Fernando Po and Lisbon. We can't fully rely on that but it's good insurance!'

I found myself taking a liking to this strangely gentle man and had to remind myself, again and again, that he was a gunrunner. At Lisbon, although he must have been exhausted, he insisted on accompanying me to the check-in and waving goodbye as I boarded the TAP flight to Rome.

* * *

Archbishop Marcel Lefebvre was the Superior General of the Spiritans. As a fellow Spiritan, I stayed with him in Rome and asked him to arrange an interview for me with the Secretary of State, Cardinal Cicognani. At that time, Lefebvre was very popular, influential and highly respected in the Vatican. Later on, he had serious difficulties with the church because of his extremely conservative theology and his stand on the Latin Mass. He had a complex personality, a rare mixture of kindness, warmth and humanity together with an uncompromising, rigid and inflexible mentality. When I went to the Vatican with him, the Swiss Guards stood smartly at attention, saluting him. Every Vatican official whom we met greeted him warmly.

It was my first time to visit the Vatican and everything seemed so far removed from life in Biafra. I felt that I was on another planet. Everything I saw dazzled me, especially the palatial buildings of the Vatican with their plush, gilded furniture, oil paintings and marble staircases.

Lefebvre and I were asked to wait in a room until Cicognani was free to see us. After some time he entered the room, dressed in a cassock with crimson buttons to match the sash around his waist. He had an intimidating presence that radiated authority and tradition. His wrinkled face, stooped body and halting pace suggested that he was well advanced in years.

The cardinal greeted Lefebvre in a brotherly fashion. I was then introduced and he addressed me sternly:

'Father Byrne, why have you left your mission to come here? I would have thought that your ministry is urgently needed in your diocese where there's much work to be done and priests are very scarce.'

I interpreted that statement as a rebuff but was determined not to let it upset me. I replied on the basis of obedience to authority which I felt would appeal to Cicognani:

'Your Excellency, it's true that there is much work to be done in my diocese and priests are very scarce there. However, it's also true that I'm bound to obey my archbishop. I'm here in Rome because he asked me to bring an important letter which the Biafran bishops have written to his Holiness, the Pope.'

Cicognani blinked and, with piercing eyes, stared at me for a few moments. I handed him the letter and, to my astonishment, he opened it. Then I realised that he must have been authorised by the Pope to open such letters. He read the letter slowly with his lips moving soundlessly. The second reading was slower, more cautious, giving greater consideration to each word. Then he took a red nib pen from the tray in front of him on his desk, read again even more slowly as he drew red lines under some words and passages.

He raised his thick bushy eyebrows and grunted a few times, his eyes firmly riveted on me: 'Father Byrne, I want you to understand that the situation of the church in Nigeria is very sensitive. For that reason I'm instructing you to do nothing, absolutely nothing. I hope you understand. Don't talk to the press, don't discuss with anyone why you are here. I want you to report every morning to Monsignor Ernesto Gallina who works here in the Secretariat of State. He'll keep you instructed on what you are to do. But remember, you must be prudent and do nothing for the present. In the meantime, I'll give this letter to His Holiness.'

As I left the room his words were ringing in my ears: 'Do nothing, do nothing.' I felt down-hearted and frustrated. It was my first experience of Vatican officialdom. As instructed, I reported every day to the Secretariat of State in the Vatican. This routine continued for three weeks.

At first the Swiss Guards, dressed in their decorative light blue uniforms and carrying their halberds in their hands, interrogated me every day at the entrance. As time went on, we developed a nodding acquaintance and I could walk freely past them on my way to meet Monsignor Gallina. Gallina was a kind and gentle person. One day I spoke frankly to him:

'Ernesto, I feel like someone who is on parole reporting here every day. Cicognani treated me like a little boy telling me to keep quiet and do nothing. I didn't ask to come here. I was sent by my archbishop with a letter from the bishops of Biafra and I don't know what's going on. I'm fed up with the whole situation. I'm sick of it all.'

Gallina laughed: 'Yes, you're Irish alright, Tony, but please be patient. Cicognani is a very old man, so don't take him too seriously. You see some of my colleagues here at the Vatican think he is becoming senile. They say that he is admiring the pictures that *aren't* on the wall.'

Some of the other Vatican officials I met were not as human as Gallina. They tended to lecture me on the importance of diplomacy, about being prudent and careful not to become politically involved in the war.

Every time I heard those lectures I reacted in some way. I tried to be diplomatic and gentle, yet firm, as I reminded the monsignori that my only interest in the war was to save the lives of children and innocent civilians. The children knew nothing about diplomacy or politics, their only concern was to survive, to avoid a horrible death through starvation.

Monsignor Angelini, one of the officials, really upset me one day. All my good intentions were forgotten as I raised my voice in anger:

'Monsignor, for God's sake, let's leave all this rhetoric and lecturing aside. Can we do something, anything, to save the lives of those innocent children?'

My first few weeks experience of Vatican officials was discouraging. There were times when I felt like giving up the effort, but I soon realised that the Vatican had other officials who were compassionate, ready to leave aside diplomacy for the sake of saving lives. Gallina had already become a friend and Benelli had earned my deepest respect, not just my obedience.

Archbishop Giovanni Benelli was the Deputy Secretary of State, later a cardinal at Florence. He was a man of action with a sharp mind, decisive, and well experienced in international affairs. He called Fr Des Byrne, a fellow Spiritan who worked in Lagos, and me to a meeting which was to initiate the church's programme of aid to Nigeria and Biafra.

Benelli chaired the meeting, sitting at the end of a long polished table. Monsignor Carlo Bayer, the Secretary General of Caritas Internationalis, the Catholic organisation for relief, was present. Some of the monsignori who had lectured me on being prudent and diplomatic were also present.

Benelli was totally devoid of diplomatic rhetoric. He opened the meeting by declaring emphatically: 'It's important from the outset to understand that the mind of the Pope is that we have to do everything possible to save innocent lives on both sides of the conflict. That has to be our priority.'

This was action time. I sensed that there would be no more lectures as Benelli gave instructions in military fashion. He

called each person by their surnames, with no titles, as he
unfolded the plan of action:

'Bayer, you'll go to Lagos tomorrow and talk with senior
government officials about the Papal Peace Mission to Biafra.
Find out what their reactions would be if the papal delegates
went to Biafra *via* Lisbon. Try to assess if such a visit would
cause a breakdown between the church and the state in
Nigeria. Report to me personally as soon as you can.'

Then he turned towards Des and me: 'Byrne, you'll...'

He stopped, as Des and I looked up, together. Smiling
broadly, he turned back to Bayer: 'Your attention to detail is
admirable, Carlo. I know we emphasised the need for total
equality in our treatment of the Biafrans and Nigerians, but I
didn't expect our two men to have the same name.' He
turned to face Des directly: 'You will accompany Bayer to
Lagos. You will assist him there and continue to monitor the
situation after he returns. Is that clear?'

'Yes, your Excellency.'

Then Benelli turned to me:

'You'll go to Lisbon. Wear lay clothes and stay in a hotel.
Report to Archbishop Sensi, the Nuncio in Lisbon, and let
him know where you are. Sensi will give you instructions to
proceed with our plan. When he does this, contact the Biafran
Government officials in Lisbon and ask them to fly the papal
delegates on one of their planes to Biafra. I want you to buy a
large consignment of medicine with the help of Caritas
Portuguese and have it loaded on the plane that will fly the
delegates. Check the plane, *personally*, to make sure there are
no military supplies on it. Explain to the Biafrans that the
Vatican will not communicate directly with them because we
do not recognise their state. When the delegates have gone to
Biafra I want you to return to Rome and report to the
Secretariat of State every day. Is it clear, do you understand?'

'Yes, your Excellency.'

'I will arrange Vatican diplomatic passports for you and
Bayer. They may be useful for your mission.'

I checked into the Dom Carlos Hotel in Lisbon, and went to visit the Nuncio. An elderly man, he looked extremely nervous as he greeted me coldly:

'Father, please understand that the people in the Vatican don't realise what it is like here in Lisbon. It is extremely sensitive. The media are constantly watching us. The Portuguese Government does not want any publicity about Biafra, so I have to ask you to stay away from the Nunciature. If there is any message I'll send it to you but please don't expect me to have anything to do with this Biafran business. I have my own work and so I'll be grateful if you do not visit the Nunciature again.'

I returned to my hotel room quite upset and sent a message to Archbishop Benelli telling him that I wanted to leave Lisbon because the Nuncio was not willing to co-operate. Within a few hours, Monsignor Lorenzo Corsini, the First Secretary of the Nunciature visited me. He had a soft, friendly voice: 'Please excuse the Nuncio, Tony. He has much work to do and is rather nervous. Try to understand and don't feel upset at the way he received you.'

It was obvious that Benelli had given the Nuncio instructions to co-operate. Some days later Corsini visited me again. He looked excited: 'We have some information for you. Benelli wants you to proceed with the plan. Bayer reported from Lagos that the visit to Biafra by the delegates will not cause a major problem there.'

That was the green light I had waited for during all those long weeks.

Mr Bernard Asika was the representative of the Biafran government in Lisbon. When I asked him to arrange a flight, he seemed embarrassed: 'My government will be very pleased to know that the Papal Peace Delegates are willing to visit Biafra. We'd like to assist them but unfortunately we don't have an operational aircraft. Some of our planes have been hit by Nigerian anti-aircraft guns and others have technical problems. Why don't you see Butch Dutting in the

Tivoli Hotel. He carries supplies for us and maybe he'll be able to arrange a flight for the delegates.'

Dutting and his secretary, Tina, gave me a warm reception at his office in the Tivoli Hotel. When I told them what I wanted, Dutting seemed delighted:

'Tony, we're always ready to assist the church and to carry relief supplies to Biafra. It'll be a pleasure and honour to fly the Papal Peace Delegates.'

I looked at him in disbelief. Peace would put him out of business! I could understand him being pleased at the extra business. He might even regard it as an honour. I smiled: 'C'mon, Butch, forget the Blarney. Let's just say you're an angel of peace but I need to know how much it'll cost us.'

Dutting looked at me in surprise. He hadn't expected such a blunt approach. For just a moment, I wondered if I had been too sarcastic – even tactically. My worry disappeared as Butch suddenly broke into a broad grin. 'OK, I see you're anxious to get down to business. I'd need $35,000 to cover the costs.'

I was shocked: 'Butch, let's talk sense. There's no point in wasting time. I wouldn't pay that kind of money. It's ridiculous.'

Dutting blinked and furrowed his brow: 'But, Tony, I charge the Red Cross $40,000 and because this is a church flight I'm reducing it to $35,000.'

'Thanks, Butch, but that price is too high.'

'How much are you prepared to pay?'

'Not more than $20,000.'

'Make it $25,000.'

'Fine, can we make a contract? Remember, Butch, no military supplies, no mercenaries. The plane must be clean.'

'No problem. Tina, honey, bring a contract form.'

We signed the contract and shook hands on it. As we finished our coffees, Dutting got his own back for my earlier comment: 'You drive a tough bargain, Tony. A few crates of guns are less trouble than distinguished passengers.'

I grinned mischievously and added: 'Probably pays better, too.' With the contract safely tucked away, I got out quickly.

Monsignors Conway and Rochcau arrived in Lisbon. They were pleased that the flight was already arranged and everything ready to go. Dutting kept to the terms of the contract and was most gracious to the delegates. He even provided catering facilities for them on the long flight to Biafra *via* Portuguese Guinea, now Guinea-Bissau.

The aircraft had technical problems on the way to Biafra but after some delay in Portuguese Guinea, they arrived safely in Port Harcourt.

As instructed by Benelli, I returned to Rome when the delegates left Lisbon.

There was great joy in Biafra when the delegates arrived, especially among Catholics, whose faith was now restored in their church. The cargo of relief supplies was an important gesture. Similar visits to Nigeria and Biafra to promote peace were made later by representatives of the Presbyterian Church of Canada, the Conference of Missionary Societies and the World Council of Churches.

The papal delegates were warmly received by Colonel Ojukwu, as they had been by General Gowon. They made it abundantly clear that their mission was not political or diplomatic, nor were they taking sides in the conflict. They emphasised that they were coming in the name of the Pope to preach peace and to appeal for the cessation of violence and bloodshed.

The peace delegates made a thorough survey of the situation and reported, in detail, to the Pope. They confirmed that the starvation was truly horrific, and that more than three million people were displaced in Biafra.

The Pope was personally disturbed by the report, and spoke with great emotion about it during his Sunday morning public addresses from St Peter's Basilica. He commissioned

Caritas Internationalis, the Catholic organisation for relief, to establish a programme for the victims of the war on both sides of the conflict.

Monsignor Jean Rodhain, President of Caritas Internationalis, and Bayer were commissioned to implement the relief programme to Nigeria and Biafra. Des Byrne was asked to co-ordinate the relief programme in Nigeria and I was appointed the director of the Caritas airlift responsible to Bayer.

* * *

So much for starting at the beginning. That background information might help, but it wouldn't solve the problem. I needed to convince these Vatican officials of the new urgency of the situation. I needed permission to use those parachutes. At least, it wouldn't be difficult to convince Bayer. I felt he would grasp the situation instinctively and help me to argue the case. I looked down at my notes. Their brevity, I thought ruefully, would at least suit Bayer's style.

CHAPTER 4

Law is *for* the People

Bayer was impressive. A small man, and thin, correctly dressed, but never fussily so, he always displayed good taste. What was truly astonishing about the man was the way he combined an extraordinary compassion for ordinary people with a Teutonic capacity for efficiency and self-discipline. No matter what problems he tackled, he had the gift of always appearing relaxed, with a ready smile which put his colleagues and co-workers at their ease.

Bayer was a fast thinker, a gifted linguist, and had extraordinary managerial skills. He organised relief programmes which catered for victims of drought, famine and other natural disasters as well as victims of war. Born in East Germany in 1915, he took particular interest in planning covert ways of helping persecuted Christians in Eastern Europe and Asia. His ability to tackle all these problems simultaneously was astonishing.

Arriving in his office about 10 am, he would remove his black coat and roll up the sleeves of his dazzling white shirt – the new day's work had begun. The large pile of documents on his desk was carefully studied, each page ticked on the right hand side to show that he had read it and important points recorded in his memory. Then his co-workers were called, one by one, and clear instructions given to them on how problems should be tackled.

By 4 pm, Bayer had dealt with most of the urgent matters. Then, he unrolled his sleeves, put on his coat and drove to his apartment where he became totally relaxed, switched off. He never allowed problems to take over his life.

Bayer once explained his attitude to work: 'I don't see any sense in spending long hours working in the office, Tony. It's better to work for shorter periods with maximum concentration and good delegation.'

Bayer was convinced that the airlift had to be organised despite the absence of Nigerian consent. His strong guttural voice reflected his conviction: 'We have a moral obligation to get this airlift off the ground to save lives.'

'Hold on, Carlo, many might say we're breaking the law if we fly relief supplies to Biafra without the authorisation of the Nigerian government.'

'Nonsense. Law is there *for* the people, not people for the law. What's wrong with a fire engine breaking the speed limits or going through red traffic lights to save lives? Even if the owner forbids it, for heaven's sake tell me what's wrong with breaking into a house that's on fire, to save the lives of children? That's all we'll be doing in this airlift.'

Bayer wanted the airlift organised without delay and at the minimum cost. In order to reduce the costs he instructed me to ship relief supplies to São Tomé from Lisbon and to have them flown from São Tomé to Biafra.

Cargo space on ships from Lisbon required special permission from the Portuguese government. Caritas Portuguese arranged an interview for me with Chief of Marine Affairs, Senhor Silva De Souza who had authority to allocate space on Portuguese ships sailing to São Tomé.

Security was tight at the Ministry of the Marine and a porter took me to Senhor De Souza's office. It was an impressive office, richly carpeted, with walls covered in blue and white traditional tiles. A large Portuguese national flag was displayed at one side of a stylish mahogany desk.

De Souza came straight to the point: 'What can I do for you, Senhor Padre?'

'I need your kind assistance to have relief supplies shipped from Lisbon to São Tomé, where we can have them airlifted to Biafra.'

'Of course. Let me see now.' He stretched for a ledger on a shelf behind him. 'Yes, I could get you some space this time next year on the Uige cargo vessel. How much do you need?'

I tried to conceal my disappointment: 'Sorry, Senhor De Souza, I should have explained that the cargo is for Biafra where many innocent civilians are dying of hunger and we need to save their lives.'

'I understand perfectly.'

He lowered his head slightly, his fingers toying with a slim gold propelling pencil. Then his expression changed: 'You know, Senhor Padre, Africans are dying of starvation every day all over Africa, except in our overseas colonial territories. What can one expect if they play politics, looking for independence when they're not ready for it?'

It was difficult for me to conceal my feelings. Yet I needed space on one of his ships, the same ships that were being used to transport Portuguese personnel and equipment to fight Africans seeking independence.

I tried again to appeal to him:

'Senhor De Souza, I know it's difficult for you to meet everyone's needs but I'm asking you to give this request your special consideration because two thousand innocent children are dying every day.'

He leaned back on his chair, fixed his eyes on the ceiling and drew a deep breath: 'Please understand, I can't manufacture ships and the best I can do for you is to give you space next year on the Uige.'

I thanked him, said goodbye, and left his office in a fury. When I returned to my hotel, I phoned Bayer and told him the story.

'Don't let it upset you too much, Tony. I've one or two friends in Lisbon who owe me favours. I'll phone them.'

Two days later, the Director of Caritas Portuguese sent me a government licence authorising Caritas Internationalis to ship as much relief supplies as necessary to São Tomé!

With the sea-freight arrangements now in place, the next step was to organise regular relief flights from São Tomé to Biafra. Bayer and I had agreed that the quickest way to get flights operating would be through Butch Dutting.

I arranged to meet him at the Tivoli Hotel, as before. When we met, I struggled to keep the meeting on a strictly business basis. Dutting made constant references to the peace delegates, how happy he had been to play his part and how he would now welcome the opportunity to save children's lives.

Of course, he had still suggested a price for each flight that seemed a lot to me. I offered about a fifth of what he asked and we haggled for nearly two hours before settling on a price of $3,800 for each flight. Since no commercial airline would have even contemplated the risks involved, I had no real way of knowing whether that was a good or bad deal. But then, Butch was probably in a similar quandary!

Finally, we shook hands on the deal.

'Gee, Tony, I'm really glad we were able to come to a deal. I really meant it when I said that I'd love to help you save the kids' lives.'

'Of course you did, Butch.'

I decided to call his bluff:

'I'm sure you'd love to prove the point by doing one free flight after each six paid ones.'

He swallowed briefly. Then he smiled, leant forward and shook my hand: 'Sure, Tony, I'd be glad to.'

We signed a contract and drank to it.

Dutting went silent again for a few moments and I wondered what he was thinking: 'Is there something wrong, Butch? Have you changed your mind?'

'No, no, Tony, I guess I was just dreaming. But, if you ever want a career change, I could always use a guy like you. Come and work for me!'

Organising the airlift had been a daunting prospect at the start. Dutting's spontaneous agreement to provide one flight in seven free, had astonished me at the time. Soon there was no type of generosity that could surprise me, as many pilots and other co-workers gave up their free time, and often their hard-earned money, to help wherever it was needed most.

The first flights of the Caritas airlift left São Tomé in March 1968, but the programme got off to a slow start, with limited supplies. Early one morning, I returned from Biafra to São Tomé. In spite of a steady sea breeze, the air was lifeless, almost too hot to breathe. I couldn't sleep. Images of children and their mothers kept flashing across my mind. Frustrated, I drafted a telegram to Catholic Relief Services in New York:

'Two thousand children dying every day. For God's sake, send baby food.'

Catholic Relief Services published these words in a lengthy advertisement in the New York Times and the generous response of the American public was far beyond all expectations.

Another time when supplies were at their lowest, I sent a telegram to Oxfam in Britain: 'I lifted a starving child in Biafra; it was like lifting an empty sack.' Later on, I saw those words used on an appeal poster in Britain. The British responded as generously as the people of the other twenty nations that contributed to the programme.

Catholic Relief Services of America, in conjunction with Caritas Internationalis, asked me to launch a media appeal for Biafra in America. On arrival in New York for a three-day visit, I was given a list of television and radio interviews and speaking appointments.

One appointment was to speak to a large group of rabbis and important Jewish business people. I was told that this was one of the most important tasks I had to do. At the conference hall where the meeting was to take place, the press officer of the Catholic Relief Services gave me my instructions: 'Make it short. Be clear and factual. Use the photographs and visuals.'

As I spoke, I felt that I was making no impression on my audience. It was just another tragedy. These people had heard so many similar appeals before. Sure, they would respond with kindness and probably even with generosity to my talk, and to the poster-size photographs of Biafran children – but they had seen it all before, too many times.

However, when I showed a photograph of Igbo people queuing to be registered in Lagos, the level of interest suddenly rose. A chord had been struck and memories were recalled of their persecution during World War II, when the Nazis forced Jews to register. They were so touched by that photograph that their generosity seemed to know no bounds.

One of them, Abie Nathan, organised several shiploads of supplies, arranged delivery of them to us at São Tomé and visited Biafra himself, in a wonderful demonstration of the concern of the Jewish community.

My co-workers and I experienced this extraordinary generosity of spirit from people all around the world. Thousands gave their time to fund-raise and millions of people contributed generously. Their many kindnesses cheered and sustained us through some of the most difficult times. With such support, we would always manage – somehow!

Caritas received many specific gifts of food in São Tomé. Many of them made sensible use of surplus foods in the donor countries. Others, given with the noblest intentions, were heavy and unsuitable for airlifting. I'll never forget a consignment of banana spread, in jars, or another of mixed pickles and ketchup! The most suitable kind of food to airlift was dried stockfish – high in protein, light in weight, easy to handle and liked by the Biafrans. Meat was always a problem. There were no refrigeration facilities available in our warehouses in Biafra. The protein was badly needed but the only way of exporting meat was to airlift live sheep and goats.

They were treated humanely on the flights, but the strange surroundings had them urinating copiously all the way! Captain John Baudin was blunt: 'If that stuff gets into the electrical installations we're in big trouble. Forget about the damn goats and sheep. We're not taking them on board and that's it.'

Knowing I wasn't going to win this argument, I murmured: 'It's amazing how you guys worry more about a little goat's urine than the Nigerian flak!'

Matching the supplies, the aircraft capacities and the practical needs of the feeding centres and other relief functions was always a problem. There were a few occasions, though, where dramatic action was possible.

Fr Patrick J. O'Connor, an agricultural development expert popularly known as 'PJ', encouraged Biafrans to grow more protein foods. This was extremely difficult as people were continually moving to avoid the fighting.

PJ's plea was that 'every available inch' of land had to be cultivated. In the 'Spadeville' project, he and Br Augustine O'Keeffe demonstrated it, producing significant quantities of beans, corn, yams, millet and rice. Despite the difficulties, others followed their example. Since PJ often provided them with their seeds, he soon had to turn to Caritas for help.

São Tomé had only one shop with a copious supply of seeds. I asked the owner how much a packet of vegetable seed cost.

'Eleven escudos.'

'What would you sell a hundred packets for?'

'Let me see. I could let you have them for a thousand escudos.'

'How many packages do you have in stock?'

'Two thousand odd.'

'How much will you sell them for?'

She looked at me in perplexity:

'Do you really want to buy the whole stock?'

'Yes, of course, I need them for Biafra.'

She excused herself and consulted with her husband. He did some more calculations on paper. When she returned, she had a broad smile on her face:

'You can have them for 19,000 escudos.'

'Right, it's a deal.'

'Thank you.'

Like so many other traders in São Tomé, she benefited a lot from the airlift. The whole economy of the little island was greatly enhanced. More important, though, PJ had his seeds.

* * *

One day, I was returning to São Tomé from a meeting in Europe and bought a copy of *The Times* at Lisbon Airport. It carried a story about the arrest of Butch Dutting in Malta. When he landed there to refuel, the Maltese security officials checked his papers and found that the log book and registration numbers on the DC 7 had been forged.

What would happen to the airlift now? I felt depressed and pillowed my head on my forearms. When I lifted my head, I couldn't believe my eyes. Dutting was walking towards me. I stared at him, open-mouthed.

'Butch, I don't believe it. I have just read that you're in prison in Malta.'

Dutting put his finger to his mouth: 'Shh! Keep your voice down, Tony. Let's find a quiet corner.'

We sat at a safe distance from others in the airport.

'C'mon, Butch, what's the story? Is it true what they say in *The Times*?'

'I guess it is. I can't believe I'm here. The security boys in Malta nabbed me. The Brits asked them to nail me on charges of forgery.

My friends in Italy were great. They arranged everything neatly, simply. Two people came to my cell, dressed as prison officers, with a spare uniform for me. In the uniforms, we just walked through the prison gates and they drove me to a ship which left, almost immediately, for Lisbon. So, here I am!'

I wondered who the 'friends' were.

The flight was called and I sat beside Dutting. It was a commercial flight to São Tomé. When our meal was served, Butch appealed to me: 'Tony, my DC 7 is still impounded in Malta, I need your help to get it out.'

I roared with laughter:

'Are you crazy? Look, Butch, you've got to be joking. You can't expect me to get involved in that, can you?'

Dutting left his food untouched:

'Look, I'm trying to help the church to save children in Biafra. The least you can do is help me get that aircraft out.'

'No way, Butch. Forget it.'

Butch thought for a while and then spoke gently:

'C'mon you must help, Tony. Most of the Maltese are Catholics and, if you go there, they'll be able to convince the authorities to release the aircraft.'

'Butch, you're not listening. The answer is "no" and will remain "no".'

'I'll pay all the costs of the trip to Malta. Besides, I'll make it worthwhile for you. You need the money for the airlift, don't you?'

'My friend, money doesn't talk with me, so please drop the matter.'

I was surprised at the chill in my own voice.

'I don't ever want to hear any more about it, Butch.'

Dutting had very few aircraft. Those he had were very often damaged, undergoing repairs in Lisbon, or otherwise not available for Caritas flights, making it difficult to operate a reliable airlift. It was frustrating to have relief supplies in São Tomé and no aircraft to take them to Biafra. We needed our own aircraft and I cabled Bayer to see his reaction:

'We can't operate an airlift this way. We need reliable aircraft. I propose that we should buy our own.'

Having sent the telegram, I began to have misgivings about it, as I thought Bayer might regard it as ridiculous. I was much relieved at his reply: 'Fly to Rome and we'll discuss your proposal.'

When I arrived in Rome, he was at the airport to meet me. He looked excited: 'Tony, I know you're tired but you must fly on to Frankfurt for an interview with a German television network. Monsignor Georg Hussler, the Secretary General of

Caritas Germany, will meet you in Frankfurt and take you to the studio. Here's your ticket. Boarding is in thirty minutes, so you don't have much time.'

I looked at him in amazement: 'Carlo, what's all this about? I was never interviewed on television before. What'll I say?'

Bayer checked his watch: 'Ja, Tony, you say we should buy our own aircraft. We need money to do that. You must convince the Germans to give us money. So go ahead. Have the interview. Don't miss that flight.'

He pointed to the departure area and I flew to Frankfurt. Georg Hussler was at the airport to meet me and took me to the downtown studio. A few hours after the interview, Hussler told me that the German government had donated DM 4 million to Caritas Germany for the Nigeria-Biafra relief programme and another DM 4 million to Das Diakonische Werk, a German Protestant relief agency. When Bayer got this news, he phoned me in Frankfurt.

'Good work, Tony, our Protestant partners and ourselves will buy four Super Constellations. Air France have some for sale, so go to Paris and negotiate a good price for them.'

Pilots working for Dutting in São Tomé gave me a good idea of the value of second-hand Super Constellations. That was to prove most useful.

I visited the head office of Air France and met Jean Bessone, one of the senior managers. He seemed amazed when I told him that I wanted to buy four Super Constellations. He smiled cautiously:

'Mon Père, is this your first time to Paris?'

'No, I've been here several times visiting my sisters, who are nuns.'

'Oh, what group of nuns do they belong to?'

'The Little Sisters of the Poor, one is in Tarare and the other in Paris.'

He smiled at the news: 'I know them. They do good work with the aged.'

His secretary entered the room.

'Mon Père, please meet Mlle Marie Laurent, my secretary. She is interested in Africa and would like to speak to you.'

Mlle Laurent phoned the canteen and ordered coffee for both of us. As we sipped it, we had some chit-chat about African affairs.

After some time, Bessone re-entered the room, took his pipe from the ashtray on the desk and refilled it, tapping it down. He reached for his matches and lit the pipe casually:

'If you have finished your coffee, perhaps we could talk a little business. Our Super Constellations are in good condition and we are willing to sell them for $200,000 each.'

I was shocked. That price was much more than Dutting's pilots had said.

'Monsieur Bessone, people who should know have told me that the value of such aircraft is considerably less. Are you sure your quote is correct?'

He stared at me, left his pipe on the ashtray and removed his glasses. 'Mon Père, if you're really willing to buy four, I could let you have them for $180,000 each, but I could not let them go for anything less.'

I tried to get him to a lower price but we could not reach agreement, so that I left his office very disappointed. My sisters astonished me later, when they told me that he had checked with them – obviously while I was sipping coffee with Mlle Laurent – that I really was a priest and their brother.

Later on, I was consoled to learn from Hussler in Frankfurt that Suderflug, a German airline, was offering four DC 7 aircraft. Their price was reasonable, and, when I contacted the manager, we quickly agreed. It was a condition that I take personal responsibility for changing the registration numbers and return the aircraft papers to him, once they arrived in São Tomé.

I flew to São Tomé on one of the newly acquired DC 7s.

* * *

The Pope's mandate to Caritas had been very clear. It was essential that there was complete parity of treatment in providing relief to both Nigeria and Biafra. This was not a diplomatic nicety but the core of the church's position. We were to relieve suffering on both sides, not to become politically involved.

The situation in Nigeria was radically different from Biafra. There was no blockade. Supplies generally, not just war materials, could flow freely into Lagos by ship and there were good internal transport facilities. In much of the country, normal life could continue, with farmers following their normal cycle of planting and reaping. The state itself had substantial resources – even if they were now strained by the costs of buying foreign arms.

It was not surprising then, that the media attention, as it developed, focused on the Biafra situation with its headline-grabbing statistics – two thousand children dying every day, three million displaced – and the drama of an airlift. But there were many people suffering in Nigeria also – the wounded and displaced, people whose lives had been shattered by the war. The ebb and flow of each battle added to their numbers. Each success of the Nigerian army also brought, along with the territory they captured, many of the starving and displaced people whose basic needs we were struggling to provide in Biafra.

Fr Des Byrne directed the Caritas relief operation in Nigeria. Working through the Nigerian Red Cross, he tackled these problems with great compassion and sensitivity. Perhaps the greatest compliment to the work Des did was that he never needed to grab headlines. The job was done quietly, effectively – and unsung.

The Caritas airlift operated for six months with limited resources but a bigger organisation was needed to make the airlift more effective.

Joint Church Aid, popularly known as JCA, was established in September 1968 when the Protestant and Catholic

Churches relief agencies organised themselves in a confederation. This confederation consisted of thirty-five, mainly Catholic and Protestant, relief organisations in twenty-one countries. Many non-church relief organisations like Oxfam and Save the Children Fund also participated.

Some JCA members had a serious problem of conscience with the idea of church aircraft flying over countries without official permission. I was at a meeting of JCA in Geneva when the problem reached a critical point. It even looked as if the JCA confederation might disintegrate.

Most of the representatives of the church relief organisations would have accepted the principle that laws were there for the people but I felt sure that many of them would have difficulty with Bayer's interpretation!

In an attempt to find a way out of this difficulty, I suggested to JCA that Dutting should be given the ownership of the aircraft and the responsibility of employing crews, but their use should be reserved for JCA. In practice, that meant that Dutting would own the aircraft and would be legally responsible for the flights and crew. JCA would have complete control over the use of the aircraft and the selection of cargo. After some discussion JCA agreed.

Dutting was also happy to agree because it made him the owner of four second-hand DC 7 aircraft. In return, he agreed to reduce his charges, be responsible for maintaining the aircraft, and to recruit and employ the crews.

Soon after the arrival of the DC 7s in São Tomé, Dutting used paint and brush to change the registration numbers. Before he climbed the ladder, he asked me:

'Tony, what numbers would you like on this aircraft?'

'That's your plane, Butch, and I wouldn't like to interfere.'

Some days later, with great pride, he showed me the new log-books and papers:

'Not a bad job eh, Tony.'

It was a struggle to keep a straight face:

'I don't want to know anything about it.'

'Of course, Father.'

He was whistling as he took the papers away. The papers, and the DC 7s themselves, did look well. The airlift was making progress.

* * *

A striking aspect of the relief programme in Nigeria and Biafra was the spirit of ecumenism that prevailed. The churches left aside their theological differences and worked together, saving lives and appealing to the belligerents for 'peace by honourable negotiations in the highest African tradition.'

Catholics and Protestants, non-denominational and secular groups, were all drawn closely together as they looked after the wounded and the hungry. Once again, the horrors of war were acting as a catalyst for change, bringing out the best in people.

The International Red Cross organised a most effective and efficient airlift from the Spanish island of Fernando Po, off the Cameroon coast. Fernando Po is now part of Equatorial Guinea. Africa Concern, recently founded in Ireland, participated in the JCA airlift from São Tomé as well as operating its own very successful airlift from Gabon.

Despite these efforts, and the efforts by JCA to have as many flights as possible every night, the death rate continued to increase. About four million people in Biafra depended on the meals they received regularly in the JCA feeding centres.

Against this background, it was not surprising that the pilots, and everyone else involved in the airlift, were willing to take great risks to get the job done. The war itself made the JCA flights dangerous and risky. Deaths and injuries, caused both by military action and accidents, were inevitable.

Pastor Viggo Mollerup, Colonel Tonnes Wickman and many other JCA officials made tremendous efforts to ensure that the flights were as safe as possible for the crews. Everything was done to have the best possible insurance policies for them. The most competent international safety experts were consulted and JCA never went beyond what are known as 'calculated risks' for the flights. Despite that, however, the losses continued.

The JCA pilots were highly motivated. Thanks to Mollerup, they now had basic insurance but their salaries did not fully compensate them for such a high-risk operation.

The pilots were disciplined and had high professional standards, depending on each other for safety. Drinking was forbidden for at least four hours before take-off and, during flights, optimum procedures were followed.

Off-duty was different! They were full of fun and usually made up for the times when they couldn't drink. Over drinks, one of their favourite stories was about the time Butch was badly stuck for a pilot. One of 'the lads' had been taken ill, not long before the first flight was due to go out. Butch phoned Bob Miller, who was off-duty, in his hotel room:

'Bob, I'm stuck for a pilot. I know it's your night off, but can you help me out?'

'Sure, Butch, I'll fly, but you'll have to send a taxi to pick me up at the hotel. I'm far too plastered to drive.'

The story, and the number of drinks Bob had, grew with the retelling. They'd never have let it happen, though – they were all too proud of their flying record. But... if the pressure really came on... Bob was so highly motivated and generous... there was always a niggling doubt, fretting away in the corner of my mind, when they told that story. No, no ... Butch was too proud of his planes, anyhow!

It was only when an Oxfam chap told me the same story, with equal brio, about a Spitfire pilot during the Battle of Britain, that I realised how expertly I had been 'wound-up'.

* * *

The strong sun was making me drowsy. Looking out the window, I saw vast stretches of sand that could only be the Sahara. In a few hours, we would be in Lisbon and I felt I was making little progress with my notes. In fact, I had added nothing at all for some time. It hardly mattered, though, since the organisation of the airlift was straightforward enough. How could I explain what might happen if it stopped? How could I convince people in the tranquillity of the Vatican that only an airdrop could prevent a calamity? If I could tell the Vatican officials what it was really like at Uli, share with them the sense of urgency, of desperate need and of the dangers, it might help.

Fr Joe Prendergast had recently written a diary of a 'typical night at Uli' and had given me an early draft. It was so good, and so evocative of what really happened, that I kept it with me in my briefcase. I looked over the article again. There were plenty of useful statistics. Better still, because it had been written for a church magazine in Ireland, it had plenty of names. Names that relatives, friends and supporters at home could identify with and share an understanding of the work they did. To any official, that would make it authentic, verifiable.

If I handed the article to the officials, they might just skim through it, extract the data and statistics, and file it. Better to tell them about the 'diary', tease them with references to names and statistics and then, before I give it to them, read the entries which dramatically emphasise the present need. That way, I might get them not just to understand the situation, but to feel it.

I started marking passages carefully:

Another day is done – another night begins.

7.40 pm: A slight haze rises from the ground after the rain and the heat of the day. Clouds are low and there is no light to be seen at the airport. The occasional car crawling along on its parking lights makes no impression on the pitch blackness.

The Flight-line Officer checks and rallies his workers, the 'fatigue boys'. Fourteen World Council of Churches flights arrived last night. Sixteen Caritas planes are expected tonight with roughly 210 tons of precious medicine and foodstuffs. JCA unloading crews are on the alert, and they have fifty lorries waiting.

An air of tension and expectancy hangs over Uli, Biafra's only link with the outside world, as all eyes and ears await the first plane. The pilots, when they land, will complain at the low ceiling and yet bless it for keeping away the Nigerian fighter jets.

7.41 pm: As always, 'Glade' hears it first. It's the American C 97. A faint sound in the distance, gradually getting louder and clearer until it roars as it circles the airport. He has found the beacon, asked for permission to land, and is now making his 'final'.

Using only his instruments to gauge altitude and the beacon for direction, he is down to 500 feet, about two miles away, as he asks for the lights of the runway. He turns on the aircraft lights and the plane seems stationary, suspended in the heavens.

The runway lights are on as the light approaches slowly. Just two minutes light allowed. It roars past and touches down. Only then one realises its speed. As the tyres touch the runway, the lights go out, engines are reversed to slow the plane and Captain Gossman moves into one of the unloading bays.

'Glade' is over to meet the Captain and greet the passengers. In two minutes the unloading crews have the sacks rolling down the plane's sliding board and the lorries are already in place to take them. The speed of the turnaround will determine whether or not the plane will do a third shuttle. The crew is anxious to get off as quickly as possible in case of an air raid. 'Glade' is in the plane cajoling and encouraging.

'Move it, lads, move it', is the cry as they encourage each other. The swish of the rollers and the constant thud of the bags as they fall into the trucks are the only other indications of the feverish activity.

7.52 pm: The runway lights are on. Harry Mullin, at the other end of the airport has heard the plane circling, knows it will land at his end. As soon as the Super Constellation moves into the bay, the lorries back up.

7.58 pm: The C 97 takes off, no runway lights allowed. As soon as its wheels leave the ground, it extinguishes its own lights. 'Glade' is quite content. He insists that a plane can be unloaded in twenty minutes. Where does he get his energy? Fr Des McGlade looks younger than his 52 years. Some think him eccentric as he shakes hands with his left hand. 'Glade' doesn't talk about the wound on his right hand – or the shrapnel that he still carries in his abdomen, a memento of the first bombing raid on the airport. He has promised his friends it will be removed after the war, when he can afford the time in hospital.

8.02 pm: It's the DC 6 with Captain Johnsonn, the 'salt man'. Biafrans consider salt the most precious consignment of all. Only by spending time under the African sun can one appreciate just how necessary salt is.

The pilots don't like it. Salt corrodes the metalwork of the plane, it's heavy and slows down the unloading. No other pilot has, as yet, carried three shuttles of salt. Captain Johnsonn spent two days in Biafra and heard the pleas Biko, Nyem Nnu – Please, give me salt. Since then, he has never objected to salt. He understands.

8.16 pm: A drone is heard in the distance. It comes nearer but gets no louder. Anxious eyes gaze into the darkness above. It is now directly over the airport and the anti-aircraft guns shatter the silence of the night, confirming our suspicions. Without radar, the gunners can only fire in the general direction of the sound. They have no hope of hitting the bomber.

The 'Intruder' is a regular, if unwelcome, visitor. His plane has radar, is comfortably pressurised, and has enough fuel for four hours. The guns keep him at 12,000 feet, outside their range but at a height where accuracy is impossible. Despite the noise, the tension is electric.

The marshal, by the light of a two-battery torch, leads the Super Connie from the parking bay to the runway. It revs up in total darkness, uses the two lights under its wings as it taxies and only when it has gained speed does it turn on its full beam. At 100 feet that, too, is turned off. All that can be seen are four exhaust flames as it veers sharply right, away from the airport and the bomber. The 'Intruder' must have seen its lights but... too late, thank God.

8.35 pm: The DC 6 takes off. As its sound recedes in the distance, the regular drone of the 'Intruder' can still be heard. He's in no hurry, a master of the waiting game, well paid and the night is young. He's already looking for the next plane, his eyes checking his radar for the tell-tale spot and the ground for lights on the runway.

Our pilots, warned by the control tower of his presence, will come in as low as possible to avoid being picked up on his screen. But to land, they must have the runway lights for that brief two minutes.

8.41 pm: Another plane is distinctly heard. Airport personnel scurry to the bunkers, the drains, or lie flat in any depression available. The powerful headlights of the relief plane pierce the darkness. The runway lights are turned on. Will it never land? The approaching light seems to be interminably slow. 'Move friend, move. Don't you know the "Intruder" is positioning himself and every second is precious!'

The plane hurtles past at 120 miles an hour, touches down and the lights go out. But not quickly enough! There's a flash in the sky, the whistle of the bomb becomes a screech as it falls, the blinding flash and the deafening explosion. It sounds a bit off target.

But he's still coming! Numbers 2, 3, 4 follow in quick succession. Lie flat on the ground, hands over head and a prayer on your lips. Those were closer. Has he hit the relief plane? It can still be heard moving into the bay, its engines revving as it reverses.

'Glade' is calling the unloading crews from the bunkers, encouraging the drivers. In complete darkness the drivers back up their trucks and the unloading begins. They work in absolute silence, each one conscious of the enemy overhead, each one listening for the whistle of the next bomb. The tension is nerve-racking, even the innocent crickets seeming to emphasise the eerie silence. Then the silence is shattered as the guns open up again, their tracer bullets lighting up the sky.

Captain Steen breaks the tension:

'Just like Guy Fawkes,' he chuckles.

8.59 pm: More lights. Another plane and the 'Intruder' is directly above. The flash, the whine, the explosion – that's numbers 5, 6 and 7. He has 3 or 4 left. They fall way off target, not even in the airport. Maybe another family in the nearby village of Amorka has been wiped out. To date, five families have been killed. Why do they stay there? One farmer put it simply: 'But where can we go? If we leave our homes and our farms we'll starve. A bomb is quicker, more merciful.'

Joe Prendergast's diary for that night still had a long way to go, but I felt that what I had marked was enough to illustrate the urgency and the desperation of the situation. Certainly, I couldn't do better.

CHAPTER 5

That Black Stuff

'Here y'are, Tony, last Coke before Lisbon. We've just made our last course change – should be landing in about two hours.'

Looking out to the right, away from the bright early afternoon sun, I marvelled at the sight of the Atlantic rollers. The African coast almost paralleled our course as it gently eased the rollers into the Gibraltar Strait. Hurrying and breaking, the Atlantic seemed to be building up its strength. Soon it would renew its age-old battle, trying to force its way through the 'Gut' at Gibraltar into the relative sanctuary of the Mediterranean.

'That's Casablanca in the distance,' Skip was saying, 'in this light, it's easy to see how it got its name... I'm sorry, Tony, I can't keep this up. We'll be in Lisbon in a couple of hours and I'll be hopping mad with myself if we've spent the time just talking about the scenery.'

'What's the problem, Skip. Can I help?'

'Yes, you can. Henry told us that he spoke to you about an airdrop and I guess we're all mystified at your reaction. Dammit, Tony, we know there are 8,000 parachutes just sitting there in São Tomé. For the life of us, we can't figure out why you're going to Europe. It's obvious that an airdrop has to be organised immediately. You're needed in São Tomé, now, to set it up.'

I was furious with myself for inviting the comment. I tried to fall back on old-fashioned bluster: 'I don't have to explain...'

'No. You don't,' Skip interrupted. 'But if you don't know that we're on your side, you have an even bigger problem than I thought.'

We glared at each other for a few moments, each astonished at the other's reaction. Gradually, I realised how preoccupied I had become about the Vatican officials and that my loyalties were no longer a simple matter. These chaps deserved my loyalty, too: 'I'm sorry, Skip. It really isn't that simple. The truth is I'd welcome the opportunity to talk about it but I'd need your assurance that it doesn't go further than the three of you. OK?'

'Of course, Tony, you can rely on that. Listen, I'm sorry about the gibe that you're needed in São Tomé.'

'Oh that! Well you're in good company there. The first time I met the Secretary of State at the Vatican, Cardinal Cicognani, he gave me a lecture on the same lines – tried to make me feel like I had deserted my post in Biafra to strut about the Vatican. I would have loved to snap at him, too!'

'The reason I'm going to the Vatican, Skip, is to try to persuade them to allow an airdrop. I've been specifically forbidden to use the parachutes...'

'But that's ridiculous. It's obvious that an airdrop is the only way now. Banning the use of parachutes is like sentencing these kids to death by starvation...'

'Hold on, Skip. There's nothing obvious about it. If I've learnt one thing in the last two years, it's that nothing is obvious in war. I'm in favour of an airdrop, and I'll try to persuade my superiors but, at the end of that, I have to do what I'm told.'

'Come off it, Tony, of course it's obvious. If these guys want to sit in their ivory towers and do nothing, we can't stop them. But don't try to justify it. It won't wash with me – or with any of the pilots who carried sick kids from Biafra to São Tomé. We know what's involved. We've carried the healthy kids back, too. It's damned obvious to us.'

'Cool it, Skip. I know how you feel but it doesn't help. This whole business of the airlift started when the Pope decided that our priority was to save lives. Archbishop Benelli set out the ground-rules to implement the Pope's wishes – including a rule that we must not use quasi-military equipment. Believe me, without Benelli and Monsignor Bayer there would have been no airlift at all.'

'I have to follow their instructions, Skip. It's my job, my commitment. But it's more than that. Remember that without the Pope there would have been no airlift. The Vatican stamped on a lot of peoples' corns to get it started. I've learned to respect people like Benelli and Bayer and, if they say that we're not to use parachutes, they will probably be right.'

'For God's sake, how can parachutes be regarded as "quasi-military" equipment in this day and age? It's obvious that their only use in these circumstances would be to save life.'

'As I said, Skip, there's nothing obvious any more. Not to me, anyhow. I cringe when I think how naïve I was, even a year ago. It seemed obvious to me that it was more sensible to send in seeds and fertilisers instead of food, wherever possible. With our loads limited by weight, seeds and fertilisers could produce many times their own weight in food. It was simple, obvious. It never occurred to me – or anyone around me, apparently – that some of the fertilisers would be used to make explosives. When people in Biafra asked for more fertilisers, I was delighted with their sensible use of resources!

When we had to limit the supply of fertilisers, it seemed cruel. Even after we cut back the amounts, I felt sure that some was hijacked for explosives. Probably not much, but some. Any was too much. No, Skip, I don't trust the obvious any more. I'll argue all I know how for the airdrop, because I think it's right, but I'll accept the decision.'

After a strained silence, Skip said: 'Is there any way we can help?'

'Maybe you have, already. You're certainly helping me to clarify my own thoughts. I want to put together my strongest arguments in favour of the airdrop. I have a lot of ideas but, to be honest, I don't know which would be the most convincing.'

'I know what I'd say. I'd just tell them about the kids. Tony, I'd spare them nothing. Tell them what the kids are like on their

way to São Tomé – and what they're like coming back. Tell
them how fantastic it is to see them bounce back, as if none of
the awfulness had happened. Tell them that they're real kids,
just the same as the boys and girls we grew up with at home,
with the same sense of fun and mischief as any of us had at their
age. After all that's happened, we can't let them starve now.'

* * *

The village was not too far from Ihiala. A small group of
women working together in a field waved cheerily and called
greetings. Instinctively, I slowed the car to a crawl and rolled
down the remaining windows as I replied. It might have been
any of a hundred villages in the area.

It had been pleasant driving out from Onitsha in the early
morning atmosphere and I was looking forward to this
Saturday morning chat with Harry Mullin. Harry had a small
mission here and also taught in the seminary. I was much too
early and, on impulse, parked the car on the far side of the village from Harry's mission.

A short walk brought me to the centre of the village.
Everyone I met had a greeting for me – mainly mothers going
to work in their fields or the markets with their baskets of
goods. A few women were sewing outside their houses, lilt-
ing a tune in time with the rattle of their sewing machines as
they hurried to complete a dress ordered by one of the other
women. One of them called me over: 'Good morning, Father,
and how are you today?'

'I'm very well, mama, and how are you?'

She smiled broadly, clearly pleased that I had used the
honorific 'mama'.

'Oh, I'm very well but my son is looking out for you. Fr
Mullin told him to tell you that he had to go to another village for a while but he'd be back soon. My son has gone to the
stream for water. He'll be back soon, too. You must rest here
while you wait for Fr Mullin.'

Beside her, a paw-paw and an orange tree had plenty of fruit

still on them. At a glance, I could see that most of the houses
had fruit trees, too. As well as the paw-paws and oranges, there
were some mangoes and the odd grapefruit. While she was
speaking, 'mama' had carefully selected an orange from the
tree, peeled it in a few well-practised movements and sliced
its top off.

'Welcome, Father. Here's a fine orange. It will clear the
dust from your throat after your journey.'

I took the orange, squeezed it gently and took a sip of the
juice. Straight from the tree, it was delicious: 'Thank you,
mama, it's very good. I think I'll sit for a while under the big
mango tree and just watch the children play. I'm sure Fr
Mullin will find me there and you need to finish that beautiful
dress.'

'Don't mind about that. It'll be finished soon enough! But
there is better shade under the mango tree. It's the favourite
spot for most of the men. I'm sure some of them will join you.
I like to watch the children playing, too. They're a great blessing to us all.'

'They are indeed, mama,' I said, waving as I moved on.

A little further on a man greeted me. He was not yet old
but relaxed in front of his house, leisurely working a chew-
ing-stick deftly from one corner of his mouth to the other. As I
approached, he took it out to speak again:

'Most of the men have gone hunting to-day, Father, although I think it's a waste of time. In my youth, now, it was
worth it. There were many more animals worth hunting then,
and we needed the food. With the crops we have today, fishing is enough. Better to leave the animals until we need them.'

I smiled and agreed pleasantly but wondered to myself
whether he preferred to conserve his energy or the animals!

The mango tree was in a corner of the open space at the
heart of the village. I guessed it was about sixteen or seventeen metres high – a very old tree. Small children were playing everywhere while their bigger brothers and sisters were
still returning from the stream with buckets and tins of water,

most of them balanced on their heads. I wondered again at
the easy grace with which they instinctively balanced their
loads.

As I sat down, I became intrigued with the actions of two
young boys, scarcely more than four-year-olds, near me.
They were working their way in my direction, taking it in
turns to wave a small milk tin on the end of a string.

With a start, I realised they had made their own thurible
and were 'incensing' everything and everyone! They had
probably watched Harry incensing the altar in the church
during festive ceremonies. In due course they reached me
and duly swung their thurible to 'incense' me.

'Who made this wonderful thurible? Tell me how it was
made.'

'Moses made it. He's the Chief's son.'

'No, Father, we both made it,' Moses said firmly. 'Joseph
made the holes in the can and I knotted the string. That's why
we take it in turns. It looks like the one Fr Mullin uses in the
church and we can swing it the way he does. We don't have
any smoke, though, so we just use air instead. My "mama"
says that we can't have enough ins...iss... incensing and
blessings.'

'Well, it's a wonderful thurible. Well done, Moses and
Joseph.'

Other children started to join us. In turn, I duly admired
all their trucks and cars made from cardboard boxes which
were pulled along the sandy road for my inspection. There
were small model bicycles, too, made from the spokes of old
wheels. Other boys displayed their adroitness with a form of
marbles that they played with large berries picked from wild
plants.

Soon they joined other boys who had started a football
match some fifty metres away. It seemed like all the boys in
the village were playing. Their 'pitch' had goals permanently
marked by small piles of stones. For a moment, the bright-
yellow ball seemed strange but then I realised that the boys

had found a good use for the bitter grapefruit which no one liked to eat. At least they made good footballs.

When I arrived, there had been small groups of boys and girls scattered in groups everywhere. Now the girls moved over towards me as they left the boys to their 'football pitch'. Clearly, it was an amicable and regular arrangement, requiring no speeches or negotiations!

A group of four young girls were nearest me now. They faced each other, holding their hands shoulder high. One recited a rhyme about the animals in the bush. At first she recited it slowly and then repeated the same rhyme at a faster speed. The girls started to clap their hands and stamp their feet in a variety of combinations – single, double and treble claps and stamps. As the rhythm built, other girls joined in, stamping and clapping, now to the right, now to the left, some to the left, some to the right, as they all chanted the rhyme. The rhythm was extraordinary, exciting and yet the average performer couldn't have been more than about six or seven years of age. As one chant finished, another was started as they casually went through their favourites. A woman with a baby tied to her back stood smiling at the girls. The baby moved its little bottom in time with the beat of the rhythm!

I had hardly noticed Harry join me.

'Sorry I'm late but I hope you got the message. I thought I might find you here. You know, I could listen to that rhythm all day!'

'It's fantastic, isn't it? It's not just the rhythm, though, it's the whole ambience of village life. Somehow, living in the town isn't quite the same.'

'I suppose you met Moses?'

'I did indeed. He and Joseph did a thorough job "incensing" me. How long have they been doing that?'

Harry chuckled. 'Oh that! They made that a couple of days ago, having seen it last Sunday. By tomorrow, the same milk tin and twine will be something else. Moses, though, is really something special. Everyone in the village seems to feel it.'

Less than a year later, I visited Harry again. This time, our business was urgent and I drove slowly through the village. The waves and the friendly greetings were still the same but the whole atmosphere had changed. The fruit trees were blossoming now, but the strained look on the faces of the people gave a sense of foreboding, not of promise. A crater, where once a house had stood, was evidence that the war had already touched the village, but the big old mango tree was still there, seemingly impervious to it all.

There were no young men about. This time their parents could not look forward to their return 'soon'. They weren't fishing or hunting now. Even some who should still be drawing water from the stream for their parents had been conscripted into the army. After a pitifully short couple of weeks training, they would face the might of the Nigerian army and many would never see their village again.

The young children still played in the centre of the village. Perhaps they were a little thinner, but as irrepressible as ever. The cardboard and wooden toys were still there, but now they were tanks and MiGs and AK 47s. The grapefruit, that had been their footballs, were toy handgrenades. The girls still chanted rhymes, too, but they were no longer about animals. Now they exhorted the young men to kill the enemy.

Although it was close to Uli, I was never to see that village again. Within months of that last visit, Port Harcourt fell and Uli airstrip was opened. Harry still worked there, but spent his nights at Uli now, unloading precious cargoes of food and medicine with Des McGlade.

Moses's village was no better and no worse off than any other in Biafra. The war was impartial in its brutality. The blockade took its toll everywhere. At his age, Moses wouldn't have noticed the change in the diet, which was forced on the whole village. Gradually, the lack of protein weakened the little ones and the elderly. The feeding stations helped but, in time, the dreaded kwashiorkor affected all the children.

Some recovered quickly in one of the local hospitals or the clinics attached to the feeding centres. Good food worked wonders – for some. Others needed urgent blood transfusions and intensive care. They were selected by JCA workers for special treatment and recuperation in São Tomé or Libreville. Moses became extremely ill and was sent to São Tomé. This little chap was far too ill to notice his first aeroplane journey or to feel the trauma of leaving home for the first time. Television crews filmed the traumatic condition of Moses and thousands of children like him.

As the pictures beamed around the world, people reacted in horror.

Caritas Germany and its Protestant counterpart, Das Diakonische Werk, established and maintained the special children's hospitals in São Tomé and Libreville. Caritas Austria shared in their establishment by sending a pre-fabricated hospital to São Tomé and a team of Austrian volunteers to construct it. Irish missionary sisters came from Biafra to assist local staff in these special hospitals. Over 5,000 children were treated and saved.

The most heart-breaking job for church workers was to select the children for São Tomé and Libreville. Priority had to be given to those who were likely to survive the flights. It was almost like choosing who would live – or who would die. Each child received an identification wristband with his or her name, and that of the home village, written on it with indelible ink. Detailed records of the children were meticulously kept by JCA workers.

The children were wrapped in blankets, placed on inflated mattresses and strapped to the floor of the aircraft. Everyone hoped and many prayed that the planes would not be shot down. Thankfully that did not happen. Ambulances, doctors and nurses were waiting, when the aircraft arrived in São Tomé or Libreville, to rush the children to the hospitals, where they received excellent medical care.

When they first arrived in the hospitals, these dying children, just one to six years old, showed no interest in food. After intensive medical care, they started to eat solid foods again.

Very few children died. It was interesting to watch how they behaved as they recovered. Fearing scarcity of food, at first they would eat some and hide the rest. Once they realised that there was no scarcity of food, they would eat what they wanted and leave the rest. As they continued to improve, they shared their food with the new arrivals and encouraged them to eat.

Medical specialists in Europe expected these children to be brain-damaged as a result of their traumatic experience in Biafra. Later, when the specialists visited the hospital in São Tomé, they expressed amazement that the children showed no signs of either brain damage or psychological problems.

As the children recovered, they organised their own meetings to discuss their problems. At one of these, they elected Moses as their 'Chief'. He was, by then, an astute and highly politicised child, tall for his six years. Moses led the children in victory war-songs and trained them to march like soldiers. When the children recovered fully, they became very selective about what they would eat. At one point there was a major problem when Sr Audrey, a doctor, insisted that a high-vitamin and protein spread called marmite should be put on their bread. When the children said that they didn't like it, they were told that Sr Audrey had said it was good for them and they should eat it. The children asked Chief Moses to intervene and solve this 'palaver'. He went to Sr Audrey's office looking very determined:

'Sister, I have been asked to tell you something by the children. You see, we don't like this black stuff on the bread. It doesn't taste nice and it is only for white people.'

Sr Audrey stared open-mouthed at the little boy, her eyes flashing. She had nursed him back from death to life, and now he was protesting about the marmite that she had prescribed. A sense of puzzlement could be detected in her voice as she tried to explain, as gently as she could: 'Moses, the other children and yourself have been very sick and we want to make you strong. You must understand that this marmite will make you grow big. When you go back to Biafra your parents and the other people in your village will be happy to see you looking so good.'

The Chief hesitated, blinked and chose his words carefully:

'You mean, Sister, that we children won't grow without this black stuff on our bread?'

Audrey smiled cautiously, realising that this six year old Chief was preparing to squash her argument:

'Er…, yes Moses, that's right.'

The Chief looked perturbed: 'But, Sr Audrey, I don't understand. In my country the people are strong and are beating the Nigerians in the war. They don't eat this black stuff and don't eat bread. They only eat yam and cassava.'

Audrey shrugged, uncomfortably aware that she had lost the argument. Knowing that she was out-manoeuvred she shuffled the papers on her desk and checked her watch: 'Now, Moses, you know I'm very busy. Like a good boy, go back and tell the other children that they must obey the sisters – and eat the bread with the marmite.'

The Chief left the room unconvinced. The following day, Audrey phoned me in my office, sounding quite upset: 'Tony, you'll have to come here as soon as you can. I don't know what to do. The children are on hunger strike. Moses met them last night after supper. After a long discussion, they decided to go on hunger strike.'

When I got to the hospital dining room, the children were sitting at the tables with their arms folded. Bread with marmite was piled high, untouched, on their plates. There was a deadly silence but I found it difficult not to laugh! These children had been at death's door just weeks ago. Now they were strong enough to stage a hunger strike.

Lucy Eke, a little girl of about four, began to cry. Copious tears ran down her beautiful face. I took her in my arms, cuddled her and brought her outside: 'You're all right, Lucy. Don't worry, we all love you. Tell me what's wrong.'

She struggled to explain, her voice interrupted by crying: 'I'm hungry and the Chief said that we're not to eat or drink anything because Sister is making us eat bread with that black stuff on it.'

'OK, that's no problem. I'll look after that. C'mon, I'll get you a nice orange drink and some biscuits. When you've finished, go back to the dining room and fold your arms with the others. Don't tell them you've eaten.'

She enjoyed the drink and biscuits, went into the dining room and folded her arms, as if nothing had happened. When the children left the dining room, the bread with the marmite was still piled high, untouched, on the plates. I had a meeting with the sisters. Audrey spoke first: 'We can't let the children do as they like. They need to build up their protein levels more before they can return home. Marmite is the best thing we have to do that.'

'Audrey, I'm sure we can find an alternative.'

Sr Carmel put a different view:

'Maybe we should thank God that they're well enough to go on strike. They certainly can't have any brain damage. I think it's important to rebuild their confidence along with their protein levels.'

We all agreed and I added my own gratitude for the sisters' great work. That 'black stuff' would have to go – but who would tell Moses? How would we tell him, without risking chaos?

Audrey called Moses to her office. When he arrived, he looked calmly at Audrey for a moment before he spoke. It was an extraordinary look. It took me a while to recognise it as authority!

'Yes, Sister, you sent for me?'

'Moses, we have a problem, we cannot get the good foods that were once plentiful in Biafra, so we have to make do with other things. With Fr Tony's help, we will get different things to eat, so that there will be no black stuff on the bread from now on. If we can't always get things that the children like, will you, as their Chief, help me to get them to eat what we have?'

'Of course, Sister, that's fine', he replied. 'I knew that by speaking to you, the palaver would finish. I'll tell the other children what we agreed.'

Peace was restored, with dignity. No black stuff. As the door closed behind Moses, Audrey realised that we still had a lot to learn about negotiation.

Constantly on the alert for a possible invasion or uprising, the Governor of São Tomé ruled the prison island with an iron fist. Before his appointment as governor, His Excellency Major Antonio Jorge da Silva Sebastiao had an outstanding military and secret intelligence career. He insisted that I should report to him every morning on the airlift and on developments in Biafra.

His palace had many of the trappings of royalty. Decorated soldiers in ceremonial uniforms guarded the palace night and day. The changing of the guard could rival the ceremony at London's Buckingham Palace. At sunrise and sunset, the Portuguese national anthem was played with great pomp and solemnity as the flag was raised and struck. Vehicles had to stop, their occupants get out and face the flag reverently.

The governor loved the status that went with his position. A kind man, with a great love of children, he was a regular visitor at the hospital. Some of his assistants, however, saw to it that the Portuguese government gained handsomely from the airlift. Port charges, and taxes on everything needed for the relief programme, greatly enhanced the government's coffers. Pilots believed that the landing fees and the price of aviation fuel were the highest in the world.

The airlift created an economic boom for the island's shopkeepers, caterers and hoteliers. It would not continue for ever so they maximised their profits while it lasted. Prices soared out of all proportion.

One day, the governor summoned me to a special meeting in his palace. Coffee was served and, as we sipped it, an assistant spoke in an officious tone: 'Senhor Padre, the Portuguese government is concerned about the large number of foreigners on this island. The government is also concerned about the Biafran children who came here very ill but are now recovered and staying in the hospital. We fear that all these foreigners may destabilise the islanders. For that reason, we are reminding you that all relief workers and crews must have valid visas. We want you to arrange the repatriation of the children to Biafra. You are free to replace them with other Biafran children who need intensive care. However, we should inform you that there will be a government levy of three US dollars per day for each child in the hospital.'

It was difficult to conceal my vexation:

'Your Excellency, the churches are very grateful to the Portuguese government for its continued support of the airlift. I appreciate your concern at the large number of foreigners on the island but, I assure you, our church relief workers and crews have valid visas. May I point out that Caritas Internationalis and Das Diakonische Werk have very limited funds and they find it difficult to maintain the children's hospital. For that reason, it will not be possible for them to pay this tax.'

The assistant looked at the governor, whose eyes twitched as he sat nervously on his swivel chair. The tension was palpable. The governor pointed a finger at me: 'Senhor Padre, I wish to remind you and other relief people that you are the guests of the Portuguese government on this island. You've no right to dictate the taxes we can levy on foreigners.'

'I'm sorry, your Excellency, but this new tax would be a serious problem. We must rethink our position about the hospital. I must refer this matter to my superiors in Rome.'

I phoned Bayer and he became very upset.

'Tony, this is unbelievable. They're making a lot of money on this airlift but they will not make money on sick and dying children. We'll close the hospital rather than pay this money.'

'The Portuguese government isn't easy to manage, Carlo. It's all powerful and can call the shots.'

Bayer thought for a while. When he spoke again, there was a coldness in his voice that was totally unfamiliar:

'So can I. I'll ask Benelli to write a letter to the governor. We'll send a copy to the Portuguese Ambassador to the Vatican and their Minister for Foreign Affairs. When you deliver the letter, make sure he's aware of the copies. He'll know the copies arrived first.'

'All the letter need do is thank the governor for his co-operation and say that the church hopes that the good relationship between the relief workers and the government will continue. That should be enough.'

When I presented the letter from Benelli, the governor read it slowly, noting who had copies, then he bowed his head in silence for a moment.

'Senhor Padre, there's no trouble, we're all Catholics here and we wouldn't like to have bad feelings with the Vatican. We won't insist on this new tax.'

I thanked him and left the palace marvelling at Bayer's tactics. Diplomacy could be useful, after all.

It was just a short time later that we gathered at the airport one evening to see a group of children going home. Of course, some of the adults watching had reservations and doubts about the children's future well-being and questioned the wisdom of their going back until the war was over. The children had no doubts. They were going home to see their parents, their village, their brothers and sisters, they were going on an aeroplane and it was great! Their excitement was infectious as they ran about, each clutching their high-protein parcel and toys given to them by the governor.

Audrey and I were chatting near the aircraft when a small group came over to say goodbye. Lucy Eke threw her arms around each of us in turn, giving each of us a hug the way only a four-year-old can.

The Chief, as we now always referred to Moses, was more reserved. He shook hands with each of us, thanking us on behalf of all the children. As they went towards the aircraft, he had a protective arm on Lucy's shoulder.

The high-protein parcels, to be given to their mothers, would supplement their food at home. They were a standard pack. Each contained some salt, of course, meat cubes and other soup-enhancers, tins of fish and other high protein foods, and a small jar of ... marmite!

Audrey winked at me: 'At least, we won't be there when the Chief finds it!'

* * *

Henry's voice came over the public address system:

'Please fasten your seat belt, Tony, we'll be landing in Lisbon in five minutes. I'm sure you'll be glad to get out of the aircraft. If you're not too tired after the long haul, you'll be welcome to join us for a nice meal in Lisbon airport. The food's good there.'

CHAPTER 6

All sorts of Bravery

The waiter drummed his pen impatiently on his order pad.
Even if we had explained, he could never have understood
the simple delight we felt as we sat in the airport restaurant,
iced drinks in hand, reading the bewildering array of choices
available on the elaborate menu. We settled on one of the two
Portuguese favourites – dobrada and bacalhau com natas.

As soon as the waiter had taken the order, the crew got
down to discussing plans. The aircraft would take three days
to repair – three days for the crew to relax and unwind.
Would they go 'on the town' tonight and then sleep for two
days – or the other way round? Just the feeling that they were
free to do as they pleased for a few days was enough.

When the meal was served, we concentrated quietly on
the excellent food. After a while, Henry left down his knife
and fork: 'I got a letter from home just before we left.
Apparently, some folks are beginning to say I'm a gun runner! They're listening to all this damn nonsense about the
church flying ammunition to Biafra. I guess none of us would
carry hardware for any money. Those damn media people
twist everything around.'

Henry was getting really upset. I tried to help: 'There's no
point in letting it get to you, Henry. Your folks know the score.
These people aren't interested in the truth. Just ignore them.'

'But, Tony, you can't let them get away with it. Goddammit,
the observers fine-comb the loads so carefully. No ammunition *could* get on our flights with those guys checking the
cargo.'

'I know they're thorough. It costs us a small fortune to have them there.'

Henry lifted his knife and fork and returned to his dobrada. After a little while, the twinkle in his eye returned: 'Do you remember the fight we had when you wanted us to carry petrol for the relief trucks? We refused the barrels because petrol was quasi-military cargo. Gee, Tony, your Irish really came out then. I've never seen you so mad!'

I smiled: 'I couldn't do a thing about it. You fellows had the upper hand. Thank God you let us take fuel from the aircraft tanks, despite the fire risk.'

'You can say that again – the thank God bit! It sure was risky but I guess everyone was very careful. At least there hasn't been an accident – so far.'

With an elaborate wink to me, Skip changed the subject.

'What's the bacalhau like, Tony? It looks interesting.'

'All these fish dishes are nice, Skip, but the mushrooms and cream make this a bit of a feast. I was quite hungry. How's your dobrada?'

'The sauce on this is quite rich, too. I wouldn't normally ask for fish, if there's a choice, but the fish is always special in Lisbon. Is yours OK, Lar?'

'Oh! Grand, grand. I was hungry, too.'

Larry was mystified when we all dissolved in laughter. With the elaborate presentation, he hadn't realised that the bacalhau he was eating was dried cod – the stockfish that he had vowed never to look at again! As we unwound over the meal, the war seemed further away, for a while.

Evening fell and we left the airport, hailing a cab to the Dom Carlos Hotel. I, at least, hoped to have a quiet night! On arrival at the hotel, I made my flight reservation to Rome for the next day, cabled Bayer advising my arrival time and requested him to arrange an interview with Benelli.

After a hot bath, I lay on the bed. The peaceful surroundings were a real luxury but I couldn't relax. It wouldn't have

occurred to me, then, that I was worrying or that the stress of
the previous months was taking its toll. That, I believed,
could happen to other people, not to me.

As the airlift gained momentum, it seemed the criticisms
grew with it. It was natural that colleagues in the front line of
the relief effort, in the feeding centres and hospitals, should
demand more supplies and an ever greater effort from us. I
suppose it was just as natural that those who wanted us to
fail should try to undermine the airlift any way they could.
The media experts told us not to deny false reports, it only
gave them more publicity. In time, we might be able to see
such criticisms as a back-handed compliment to the effective-
ness of the airlift, but not yet!

Sleep was impossible for a long time as I analysed and
reviewed the many criticisms and the serious crises that we
had faced during the airlift.

* * *

Lord Fenner Brockway and Frank Allaun MP arrived at my
office in São Tomé. Brockway was a noted humanitarian, in
his sixties, whose powers of persuasion in settling party
squabbles and solving industrial disputes had given him
political prominence. His political enemies saw him as a wily
old fox, not easy to out-wit.

After a short preamble I said:

'Gentlemen, you're welcome. I hear that you've visited
Lagos and had some discussions about peace-making.'

'Yes, Padre, we've one thing in common with you. We
want peace in this war-torn country. It's the only real way to
save the lives of innocent civilians. The discussions Mr
Allaun and I had last week in Nigeria were promising but we
must see the political leaders in Biafra. We need your help to
fly there.'

I emphasised the danger: 'There's no problem about flying on one of our aircraft, you'll be more than welcome.
However, we can't take responsibility for your safety. You
have to understand there are serious risks involved.'

Brockway smiled assuredly: 'I realise that, but the Nigerian authorities have given me a guarantee that there will be no bombing at the airport when we fly in and out of Uli.'

'That sounds good, but how will they know when you're flying?'

Brockway handed me a note: 'I would be grateful if you would send this cable to Lagos two days before I fly in and out of Uli.'

The note had a typed message on it. I couldn't make sense of it. He saw the puzzlement on my face, but waited for a moment while I wrestled with the message, before he added: 'Of course, it's coded.'

I arranged everything as he had requested. My co-workers in São Tomé went into top gear, thrilled at the opportunity of four safe flying nights at Uli. On the nights designated by Brockway and Allaun to fly in and out of Biafra, our planes made the maximum number of trips, with maximum cargoes. It was a terrific opportunity to get in salt and other awkward loads.

The night the two parliamentarians flew to Biafra was a Caritas night at Uli. BBC news reported that the Caritas flights had carried ammunition that night, probably unaware that Brockway and Allaun were on board one of the aircraft. When they returned, Brockway shook hands warmly:

'Padre, I'm deeply grateful for your assistance. We'd never have made Biafra without your help.'

'Welcome back! I'm happy you had a safe visit but I'm sorry to say the media have you in trouble. The news isn't good about you.'

'What's wrong? What are they saying about us?'

'The BBC say you flew to Biafra on a church flight loaded with weapons.'

Brockway was aghast.

'Damn nonsense! By George, it's scandalous and I can prove it. I'm still smelling from that dreadful stockfish. I assure you, padre, I'll do something about this lie, take them to the cleaners for it. Mark my words.'

'I hope you do. We're tired of these false accusations but there's very little we can do about them.'

'Fortunately, I can! I'll take it up as soon as I arrive in London and let you know the result.'

A short time after his return to London he cabled me, saying that he had demanded a transcript of the false BBC report but regretted that his legal advisers believed the report was not libellous. The legal language used would protect it – 'it was reported that arms were carried on the Caritas flights.'

Perhaps all the advisors were right, but it hurt!

The BBC has never corrected that report.

Newspaper reports accusing the churches of flying mercenaries to Biafra were just as untrue. They were never allowed on JCA flights. Even when the Biafran government flew some of them to São Tomé for a break, church relief workers chose to keep a safe distance from them!

One night, after the last flight had departed for Biafra, I sat with a group of relief workers in the airport bar. A mercenary on his holiday break came over to me:

'Père Byrne, excuse me. Do you mind if I have a few words?'

I felt I couldn't reasonably refuse to speak to him but my response was cold, calculated not to encourage him: 'What is it?'

He gestured to some easy chairs: 'Mon Père, my name is Pierre from France. I'm in charge of the Biafran Commandos.'

I stared at him. Standing six-foot tall, muscular and hard-faced, he looked vicious and brutal with bloodshot, narrowed eyes. In his mid-thirties, he was dressed in a faded grey safari jacket, scuffed blue jeans with large fastened pockets on each leg. His brown jackboots were dusty.

As we sat down, he tossed back his whiskey and called the bar attendant: 'Another double, please. What will you have?'

'Thanks, I'm OK.'

He removed two large Havana cigars from his inside breast pocket: 'Fancy one?'

'Thanks, Pierre, I don't smoke.'

He lit the cigar slowly and picked his discoloured teeth with the spent match. As he pulled on the cigar and sipped his whiskey, he fiddled with the box of matches.

'I'm tired training these commandos. It's not easy. They're the only real soldiers in Biafra.'

'What kind of training do you give them, Pierre?'

'I use a simple method. Before starting, I line up twelve trainees... call one of them to me...'

Then he stopped talking, sighed as he took a match from a box. He held it between his open forefingers and then broke it with his thumb. He pulled hard again on his cigar: 'I shoot him dead through the eyes. Then I tell the other eleven that they'll receive the same treatment, if they attempt to retreat from the front-line. After that, I start the training programme.'

My stomach turned at the thought of such savagery. I swallowed hard: 'Pierre, are you proud of what you do?'

He looked uncomfortable with my question.

'I have no qualms about what I do and I'm well paid for it. You see, I love the Biafran kids. I've adopted one, Claudette, a real little angel. She lives in France with Jeanne, my companion. I want to save the other kids and the only way to do that is to train the commandos to fight the enemy and win the war.'

There was a long silence. I stood up to close the conversation.

'Just a moment, Père Byrne. I haven't come to the point yet.' He lifted his glass and took a mouthful of whiskey. 'You know your church people in Biafra are always in danger. I've trained my commandos to respect them always and to defend them when they're in trouble.'

'Thanks, Pierre. I appreciate that.'

Then he thought for a while, studied his dirty fingernails and cleared his throat:

'I have a problem. I need your help. I've just received information from our intelligence unit that the Nigerian forces are advancing into the heart of Biafra. I've been instructed to

cut short my holiday and return immediately to train as
many commandos as possible.'

He pulled on his cigar:

'The Biafrans won't have a flight for a few days but I must
get back now. Please let me fly on one of your aircraft.'

I looked at him intently for a second:

'Sorry, Pierre, no way. You know mercenaries are not
allowed on church flights.'

Anger flared in his face. He raised an admonitory finger at
me and shouted a stream of obscenities:

'By God, Byrne, I'll rape every one of your damn nuns
when I get to Biafra. What's more, I'll order my commandos
to do the same.'

As I turned to rejoin my friends, I smiled derisively at him:

'But of course, Pierre, you're a brave military man.'

During one of my visits to Biafra, my unpopularity became
evident when I met a group of missionaries. One of them
aired his feelings: 'Byrne, you're OK in São Tomé. You've plenty
of food and drink, but I wonder if you know what's happening here. We have to look at starving and dying people every
day and we don't understand why you don't send more supplies. What you're sending us is far too little.'

I tried to keep cool. It was easy to understand his frustration in the face of their needs, so I tried to explain our limit-
ations as patiently as possible.

'My friend, the maximum payload for most of our aircraft
is ten-and-a-half tons. We can't possibly airlift enough supplies to feed all the starving people. Besides, we're not the
World Bank. We have very limited funds.'

Many of those present shrugged their shoulders irritably
in disbelief. As tempers became frayed, one of them spoke
angrily: 'If relief people like you had fewer conferences in
Europe and America, we'd have more supplies.'

I took a few deep breaths, biting my lips in an effort to stem
annoyance: 'Look, I know you fellows are agitated by this

horrific situation. We all are. But try to realise that we're a small outfit. Let's not get into a messianic complex. We can only do what we can do. We can't work miracles.'

I was just as unpopular with Biafran officials because the church aircraft wouldn't fly them to Uli. We insisted that they should fly on Biafran government planes. They were also annoyed at our refusal to carry weapons, luxury foods or goods for state functions in Biafra.

The churches were constantly criticised for keeping Biafra alive. I argued several times during television interviews that the churches were not keeping Biafra alive as such. What we kept alive were many people at risk, innocent civilians who happened to live in a country called Biafra. They had a right to life. They didn't start the war. They were its victims.

Mr Dominic Sanusi, a friend of mine in the Nigerian Ministry of Home Affairs, was worried about my safety. He wrote to me, via a contact in Europe, feeling that he should warn me:

'Tony, please be careful. You're fourth on the wanted list in Nigeria. If you're captured, they will kill you.'

That made me feel nervous. I had tried to put a brave face on it by saying that I often felt needed in Africa – but to feel wanted was a great compliment.

Some of my cynical friends argued that the first three on the list must have been extremely unsavoury characters!

* * *

For five nights in August 1968, church flights couldn't land at Uli. The Nigerians had acquired radar controlled anti-aircraft guns, making the flights too dangerous. There were many incidents but finally, after one aircraft returned to São Tomé badly damaged, the pilots refused to fly.

During this crisis, Count Carl Gustav Von Rosen, a famous Swedish pilot, arrived in São Tomé with a crew on a relief flight chartered by Nordchurchaid, the Scandinavian Lutheran Church relief organisation.

Von Rosen had become internationally famous during the occupation of Abyssinia by Italy, 1936-1941. During the occupation, he played a significant role in bringing relief supplies, on behalf of the Red Cross, to the people of Abyssinia. After the war, Emperor Haile Selassie decorated him and commissioned him to organise the new Ethiopian airforce. He also served as a pilot in the United Nations operation in the Congo. He was a deeply religious man of sixty-five. His keen military mind seemed to be in conflict with his emotional character, making him tearful when he spoke about the children.

I appealed to him for assistance: 'Captain, no church flight has landed for the last five days in Uli. Supplies are very low and many children are at risk in Biafra. Is there anything you could do?'

His voice cracked with emotion: 'Father, I promise you before God that I will do all I can to solve the problem. First let me fly with a church pilot and find out what the real problem is. Then we'll take it from there.'

It wasn't easy to find pilots who were willing to take the risk, but Captain Roland and flight engineer Brady agreed to fly with Von Rosen. The flight encountered very heavy flak and couldn't land at Uli. On his return, Von Rosen came to my office, looking agitated.

'The church pilots aren't experienced at combat flying. They're making basic mistakes. They shouldn't use their radios or lights. That makes it too easy for the Nigerians. They must fly over as much marshy ground as possible – where the Nigerians can't position anti-aircraft guns.'

'Captain, all of that makes sense, but the crews simply refuse to fly.'

He clenched his fists and looked determined: 'I'll go myself during daytime and take the Nigerians by surprise. Flying at three or four hundred feet, I'll avoid radar detection.'

I was stunned at this: 'Are you crazy? That would be suicidal. The Biafrans would bring you down because they would think it's an enemy aircraft.'

Von Rosen relaxed now, all the uncertainty and emotion gone. This was what he knew best, risks that he understood and could calculate. 'Tony, all I need is someone to fly with me who knows the Rivers area and is well-known to the Biafrans. He can direct me on the flight and assure the people at Uli that it is a church flight.'

I thought for a while: 'Fr Bill Butler, one of my co-workers, is your man. He worked in the Rivers area. He's also a well-known educator and the Biafrans love him. Let's go meet him.'

When I introduced the two men, I explained Von Rosen's plan and asked Bill if he would help. He faced Von Rosen directly: 'Captain, you understand the risks better than any of us. If you're happy to fly, I'd be delighted to go with you. Anything to break the gloom around here would be very welcome. You've no idea how frustrating it is to watch badly needed stuff stockpiling here while there are no flights to take it.'

'If we take them by surprise, it needn't be risky, Bill. We must make sure our departure time is kept secret. How well do you know the Rivers area?'

'Like the back of my hand. Here, let me show you...'

I don't think they noticed my leaving them, they were in such intense conversation over the map.

It was strange watching them take off, in broad daylight, from São Tomé. The weather conditions were important for such a flight. The sky was high, giving clear visibility for their task, yet strangely devoid of either colour or warmth. As the aircraft faded into the distance, I hoped they were the conditions Von Rosen wanted. It might be a long, anxious wait.

The flight was a complete success and the Biafrans gave Bill, Von Rosen and the crew a warm welcome. Von Rosen's report was cryptic, concentrating on how to minimise the risks in future.

The Nigerians had been taken by surprise at the day flight and the aircraft's low altitude avoided the radar screen. The daylight flight had enabled them to determine that there were few, if any, guns in the marshlands of the delta region.

Better still, it would be very difficult for the Nigerians to put any there, even when they became aware of Von Rosen's flight plan.

Bill Butler's description of the same flight had a different emphasis! He found the flying at 150 feet or 'tree-top level' both exhilarating and terrifying.

'Tony, I prayed that he'd go up just a teeny-weeny bit higher – as I instinctively lifted my feet off the aircraft floor. Looking out the windows, I knew we were 150 or 200 feet off the ground, but you'd feel you were almost in the water, or the trees. Once I got acclimatised, I had a fabulous view of all my old Rivers haunts and it was great to be able to help Von Rosen.

'He's some pilot. Despite all the manoeuvring, his navigation was spot-on at Uli. They couldn't believe it when I spoke to Uli control. Within minutes, we were on the ground and Von Rosen asking me: "What's all the fuss about a difficult runway? That road must be at least a mile-and-a-half long and it's well tarmaced." We were mobbed at Uli. It must have been terrible there, with no idea when the next plane would arrive. Our unexpected arrival was the tonic they needed. The excitement, the euphoria and the welcome were very special. They were all out to greet us – including Gus Finucane and Joe Prendergast. We missed Glade, though. He was just arriving as we took off.

I congratulated Bill, shaking his hand warmly:

'That's fantastic. It looks like we're back in business. I'm delighted you agree that Von Rosen knows his stuff. He was astonished at how well you knew the Rivers area. He reckoned you knew the age and species of every tree – not just their locations.'

'And now I know their heights as well!'

The airlift was quickly restarted and the JCA fleet of four aircraft was soon increased to sixteen. JCA America and Can-airelief joined in, substantially increasing the airlift's capacity. The Americans introduced the C 97G Stratofreighter, which the US government had sold to them for a purely nominal consideration.

Von Rosen established new and successful flying orders. JCA aircraft flew as much as possible over the marshland areas of Nigerian-held territory. No lights of any kind were used, and no radio communications after take-off.

The pilots were an extraordinary bunch of people. Most of them normally worked for passenger or cargo airlines. They felt it was 'doing something useful' to spend their annual holidays on the airlift. Many stayed on – some arranging leave of absence, some quitting their regular jobs. Most of them had never flown in a war zone before.

For the first time, they were encouraged to think tactically. Von Rosen organised many group sessions where they sought to out-think the Nigerians and to surprise them with new and ever-changing tactics, if necessary. John Schumbach was a TWA pilot working his holidays. At one of the first sessions, he protested: 'But Carl, all we want to do is fly in some food. We don't want to get involved in that military stuff.'

Von Rosen nodded: 'I agree, but the Nigerians would argue that, by flying in relief supplies, you are involved. They're determined to shoot you down, bomb you on the ground or stop you any way they can. Sure, we want to fly in food, but we also want to fly ourselves, and our planes, back safely.'

Meikan was reflective: 'We're far too predictable. The 'Intruder' can set his watch by us. When we arrive, he bombs Uli and calls up his MiG friends. When they've finished, he dumps the rest of his bombs on Uli and goes home. All on schedule. You're right, Carl, we must vary our routines.'

As the sessions progressed, the pilots quickly learnt to anticipate Nigerian tactics and to minimise their effect. They constructed several tactics of their own, some of them purely theoretical. As Von Rosen emphasised, the main purpose was to sharpen their own thinking. Soon, there was a new confidence about the pilots, a new spring to their step.

They were a lot more ready, now.

As the airlift gained momentum, many pilots were upset by the high death rate amongst the children. Von Rosen was extremely distressed. Despite his sharp tactical mind, he was one of the most emotional people I had ever met.

He was asked not to fly to Biafra but to concentrate on his role as Chief of Flight Operations. In that capacity, I often found myself working closely with him. I felt honoured to do so but, as time went on, we had differences of opinion. Early one morning, he came to my office looking nervous and tense. His eyes were bloodshot and there was a distinct quiver in his voice:

'Tony, history is being repeated here. The Nigerians are the Nazis, and the Biafrans are the Jews. This is the Second World War all over again. We can't let this happen.'

He took his handkerchief from his pocket and wiped tears from his eyes. I couldn't agree with his analysis but I had to be sensitive to his feelings. His first wife had died in a concentration camp during World War II. I found it difficult to console him but tried to find the words:

'Captain, it's OK. Relax now a little, I know you're very distressed by the situation. Just take it easy. I know it's difficult for you. Let's have a coffee and we can talk.'

As he sipped his coffee he looked tense and disturbed. There was a long silence as he appeared to think deeply, then he held my two hands. 'Listen Tony, I've come to ask you to fly with me to my friend Emperor Haile Selassie and ask him to give armaments to Biafra to finish this war.'

I tried to conceal my shock by telling myself that this man was sincere but a victim of Biafran war propaganda and blinded by the memories of his past. This was flouting all the JCA directives he had accepted. Von Rosen stared at me as he waited for an answer. I tried to delay by putting extra sugar in my cup and stirring it slowly. He couldn't wait any longer and asked me sharply: 'Well... c'mon, tell me. Will you come with me to the Emperor or not?'

I tried to prepare my answer as Von Rosen looked fiercely

at me: 'Captain, you're a professional military man and I'm a priest. We come from two different worlds. Any political or military involvement in the war is anathema for me. I can't go with you to the Emperor.'

He was no longer pale. He was ashen grey. He stood up, pointed his finger at me and raised his voice in anger: 'Yes, we are different. Your Christianity is different to mine. I wonder is your God the same as mine. Don't you care about the two thousand children who are dying every day? For heaven's sake, Byrne, you must know the only way to stop this genocide is to help the Biafrans win the war. You couldn't be that stupid.'

He turned on his heels and stamped out of the office.

When he left, I immediately contacted the other JCA officials in São Tomé and told them that it wouldn't be possible for him to continue. He was gently asked to resign but chose to do so publicly.

When Von Rosen resigned from the church relief programme, he became more relaxed because he was not restricted by church ethics. He offered his services to the Biafrans, who commissioned him to restructure their air force. He bought a small fleet of elderly Constellation aircraft, fitted them with rocket launchers and used them to destroy Nigerian bombers on the ground in Lagos. His day-time exploits, all seemingly at treetop level to avoid radar detection, were often sensational, attracting widespread publicity.

* * *

Another major crisis in the relief programme happened when ten Italian workers were killed and fourteen others captured during a lightning attack into Nigerian territory by Biafran soldiers. These oil workers were employed by Ente Nazionale Idrocarbui (ENI), a giant energy conglomerate based in Milan.

Ten of the prisoners were Italian, three German and one Lebanese. They had been tortured and imprisoned by the Biafrans, then sentenced to death. Not surprisingly, the international community was shocked and fund-raising efforts were seriously affected.

At the time, I was in Dublin recovering after a medical procedure that hadn't been available in São Tomé. Bayer sent me a telegram: 'ENI officials will arrive in Dublin early tomorrow on their private jet to bring you to Rome. You will collect and bring to Ojukwu a letter from the Vatican requesting him to have the ENI prisoners released. See you in Rome. Greetings. Bayer.'

The ENI jet arrived. I was astonished at its luxury, compared to the DC 7s. The executive jet had sleeping accommodation and its own small kitchen with an on-board chef. The ENI officials briefed me on the details, stressing their concern. Notwithstanding this, when we arrived in Rome, I was surprised to discover that my intended visit to the Biafran government was widely published in the Italian newspapers and on television.

When I collected the letter from the Vatican, I travelled on the ENI jet to São Tomé and continued to Biafra on a church aircraft. I contacted Ojukwu's private secretary and asked for an interview. The reply was not helpful: 'I regret to inform you that, due to important State commitments, His Excellency Colonel Ojukwu will not be free to see you. If you have any important message from the Vatican, please send it to me and I will present it to His Excellency.'

The Biafran authorities were not willing to discuss the prisoners' release. It soon became clear that they were seeking the recognition of Biafra as a condition for the release of the condemned men.

The Italian government would not agree to any arrangement involving recognition and the release of prisoners. There was great disappointment in Italy at the apparent intransigence of the Biafran Government.

The headlines in Italy were blunt: 'Byrne's mission to Biafra a total failure.' Mr Eugenio Chefis, the general manager of ENI, arrived in São Tomé with some senior assistants on a second executive jet owned by the company. Chefis came to my office, looking grey and worried: 'Tony, we're very concerned about the safety of our men. They're oil workers who were simply trying to earn their living. What can we do to save them?'

'Eugenio, it's a tough time for you and your staff. I share your feelings. You know it'll be difficult to convince the Biafrans to release them. Even the appeal from Rome hasn't shown much success so far. The only suggestion I can make is that Princess Cecilia de Bourbon-Parma should be asked to intercede for them with Ojukwu. If she were to visit Biafra and explain that support for the Biafran cause in Europe is decreasing tremendously, Ojukwu might rethink his position on the prisoners.'

'Who is this Princess Cecilia, Tony? I don't know her.'

I explained that she was a member of one of the families contesting the succession to the Spanish throne. An attractive, middle-aged woman, she lived in Paris and was involved in international politics but totally dedicated to helping people in need. Naturally, she favoured her father or uncle as the future King of Spain – but that was not to be.

'Do you know her?'

'Yes, I've met her many times. She lives in Paris. I'm not sure where.'

'Please fly to Paris on one of our jets. Persuade her to visit Ojukwu. It's our only hope to save these innocent men. My colleagues in Paris will help you to find out where she lives.'

It would have been difficult to refuse. I flew to Paris that day.

At Paris, ENI officials brought me to their office. Four of them set about telephoning all the Bourbons in the directory. Eventually, they found out where Princess Cecilia lived and made an appointment for me.

When they drove me to her villa, an elderly Spanish servant ushered me into a large room. There was nothing in that room that was not simple, dignified, tasteful and, above all, there was nothing that did not exemplify the grandeur of royalty. While I waited for the Princess to arrive, I admired the elegant furnishings, carved doors, chandelier and large painted portraits.

Striking in appearance, Princess Cecilia entered the room and shook hands warmly: 'Welcome, Fr Byrne. It's good to see you again. It seems a long time since we met in São Tomé. I trust you're keeping well despite the strain of the war and the airlift.'

'Yes, thank you, Princess, but we're facing a serious problem. I'm sure you heard that the Biafrans have killed oil workers in Nigeria and condemned fourteen others to death. The Vatican has tried to intercede on their behalf but failed. I've come to ask your help in saving these innocent men's lives.'

'I don't know what I could do to help.'

'I know you enjoy the confidence of Ojukwu. Would you consider flying to Biafra and explaining the international reaction to him? If Ojukwu knew the situation in Europe, he would consider releasing the prisoners. Ojukwu must understand that the international image of Biafra has deteriorated considerably since the oilmen were killed and the death sentence imposed on the others. If nothing is done soon, it will deteriorate further. It's difficult now to raise funds for the airlift. People say that the Biafrans are oppressors and we'll have to discontinue the airlift if more donors withdraw their support.'

She bowed her head in deep thought and fingered the pendant around her neck. She was genuinely bewildered by my request:

'I think you're over-estimating my power of persuasion with Ojukwu. He can be strong-headed in his views.'

'I know, but we must explore every possibility to save the men's lives.'

'Yes, I agree, but it is not easy in this situation.'

She put her right hand to her mouth, closed her eyes and thought for a while. Then she lowered her hand from her mouth to speak: 'Yes... Well, in principle, I'm personally willing to fly to Biafra to see Ojukwu. However, I must consult

my papa and his advisers. Please return here in four hours'
time and I'll give you a final answer to your request.'

I left the villa wondering what her father and his advisers
would say.

When I returned after four hours the Princess looked relaxed but cautious. 'I'm happy to tell you that papa has given
me clearance to visit Ojukwu.'

I was relieved to hear the good news but then she dropped
her eyes, looking at the floor in embarrassment:

'Er, I'm sorry, but there's one condition which my father
has laid down. He must receive a personal letter from the
Pope requesting the family to intercede for the prisoners.'

My heart sank in disappointment. I suspected that the
Pope wouldn't write a letter that would involve the church in
the royal dispute. When I phoned Bayer, he grunted: 'Forget
it, Tony. The Vatican would never write such a request and
risk being involved in the succession conflict. No way. It
would be a waste of time asking for the letter.'

Disappointed, I returned to São Tomé after the failed effort
with Princess Cecilia. On arrival at São Tomé, I was astonished to find a message from State House requesting me to
visit Biafra with Bayer to witness the release of the ENI prisoners. The message said the prisoners were being released as
a response to the Vatican's request for clemency.

Bayer was overjoyed to hear this good news and flew immediately to São Tomé. We flew together to Uli, where Joe
Prendergast met us.

Despite the urgency, Bayer insisted on seeing how the
cargo was unloaded and greeting everyone. From there, we
drove to the make-shift prison for the handing-over of the
prisoners.

Many journalists, including Frederick Forsyth, were present for the formal ceremony. After some considerable delay
in the prison yard, the prisoners appeared, looking well but
nervous. Bayer and I signed the release documents and travelled with them to Uli. We flew on a church flight to Libreville,

Gabon, and then on to Rome on an Alitalia jet, chartered by ENI. There was an air of celebration during the flight, as the oilmen enjoyed the good Italian food and wine which they had missed so much in prison.

It all became too much for one of them, who had been their cook in Nigeria. As he recalled the deaths and the torture, he became very distressed and needed heavy sedation on the flight. Later, he was hospitalised in Italy.

After the main meal on the flight, four ENI officials asked me to join them at the back of the cabin. They looked at me rather seriously and Giorgio Torelli started the conversation: 'Tony, we're so grateful to you for what you have done. You see, we've been talking about you and your future. We would like to arrange something nice for you.'

I looked at them in puzzlement, wondering what they had in mind: 'Arrange something nice? What do you mean?'

'You see, Tony, we've been saying that it's not good for you to stay as you are. You must go up the ladder a little.'

'Up what ladder? What do you mean?'

Torelli's face was all concern and tinged with embarrassment because I did not seem to understand the suggestion he was making.

'We think you must become a bishop or a monsignor or something like that. We are ready to arrange things with the Vatican.'

When I understood what he was suggesting, I laughed loudly: 'My friends, I must explain to you. I don't want to become a bishop or a monsignor, or anything else. Thanks all the same!'

Torelli looked surprised: 'Oh Tony, now please, you can't stay like this, just as a priest. We can arrange things for you for your future.'

I felt sorry for these men who believed that money and power could call the shots. They meant well but they weren't accustomed to the way the church works. Torelli looked at me in perplexity:

'It's like this, Tony. We need to show our gratitude to you in some way so we'd like you to take a little money for all you've done.'

I was quite adamant:

'Thank you, but please understand I don't do this work for money. I appreciate your generosity, but try to understand my position.'

Torelli sighed in frustration: 'Let's discuss this amongst ourselves and we'll talk to you later, Tony.'

Forty minutes or so later, Mr Chefis, the general manager, came to me: 'Tony, would you like to join me for a drink? There's a seat beside me.'

When I sat beside him, he grinned, tapping his nose with his finger: 'My staff have told me about the discussion they had with you. ENI really want to do something to express their gratitude. You must have a lot of expenses and we would like you to accept a small gift of some money.'

There was a long silence before I responded: 'I'm grateful, Eugenio, but try to understand. I really couldn't accept your kind gift.'

He snorted gently, staring at me in frustration. Then he cleared his throat and smiled gently: 'OK, but you are involved in many projects for people in need. Please let us help some of them.'

'Thank you. That would be most acceptable.'

He handed me a card with his private address on it.

'Good. You can write to me personally at this address.'

Thousands of Italians cheered as the plane landed in Rome. Giuseppe Saragat, the President of Italy, headed the official reception in the VIP lounge. He gave a short speech of welcome to the released prisoners, then we were rushed off to the Vatican for a midnight audience with Pope Paul. It was a highly emotional experience, mixed with joy for the released prisoners and deep sorrow for their colleagues who had been killed.

Those who knew the Pope very well said that they had never seen him so visibly moved as he tried to keep back his tears during the speech made by one of the released prisoners, who thanked him for saving their lives.

Many Vatican officials attended the Papal reception for the former prisoners. As I looked around the room, I saw many who had told me during my first visit to the Vatican to 'do nothing, be prudent.'

Among them, though, was Archbishop Benelli. He embraced me warmly and gestured me to a quiet corner in the audience hall:

'Padre Byrne, I have often thought of you and prayed for your safety and that of the other missionaries involved in the relief programme. It seems such a long time since we planned the Papal Peace Mission and the airlift. There have been so many developments since then.'

I was very humbled by his concern: 'Yes, Archbishop, but only for you nothing would have happened.'

* * *

The unaccustomed luxury of the bed in the Dom Carlos was doing its job, but it was the thought of Benelli's kindness that made me relax and I drifted off to sleep.

CHAPTER 7

Direct Hit

Smiling air hostesses walked down the aisles of the aircraft, checking that everyone was both secure and comfortable for the flight to Rome. Shortly after take-off, trolleys laden with every type of drink were wheeled out and, as soon as they were cleared away, a hot lunch was served.

It was some time since I'd been offered a hot meal on an aircraft. On longer JCA flights, we were duly grateful if someone brought sandwiches. Someone usually did. The blockade, and the human cost of the relief effort to cope with it, had taught us to appreciate everything to do with food. I had to remind myself that it was the situation in Biafra that was bizarre and the luxurious, uncomplicated routine of the Alitalia flight represented the normality of peaceful times. The JCA flights were never luxurious, seldom routine.

* * *

One of the earlier flights of the airlift, to Port Harcourt, taught us a lot about operating in a war zone. We learnt that in any war, there tend to be more losses recorded as accidents than as a result of enemy action. The distinction is often academic. An accident may be caused by earlier damage but the threat of enemy action is always an underlying factor.

Captain Bill Harkins normally flew Boeing 707s. He had volunteered to fly the elderly DC 6 for the churches during his holidays. The leisurely pace and the relative simplicity of the aircraft brought back fond memories of his early flying days and he was doing something really useful, rather than just lying on a beach. The load of medicines on board would save a lot of lives.

Two passengers had joined him on the flight, Sr Jane Nolan and Fr Fintan Kilbride, experienced missionaries on their way to work in Biafra.

Number two engine was giving Bill a little cause for concern. His engineer had warned him that the engine was losing oil and he could see that the temperature was starting to creep up. It could wait. Even if he had to shut it down, the other three engines would easily take them to Port Harcourt and coming back without a load would be no problem.

The secret instructions for landing had intrigued him. The very idea of radio silence, just a coded radio signal at the last minute to request the lights and the special set-up with the radio beacons, was strange, cloak and dagger stuff. Jim, his co-pilot, had laughed at the precautions, elementary compared to his RAF days. He could look after that part.

As the aircraft descended to Port Harcourt, it was coming into some disturbed weather. The tropical squall didn't amount to much, but Bill felt he should warn his passengers. He reached for the intercom switch: 'Please fasten your seatbelts. We should be landing in about twenty minutes but we'll be experiencing some turbulence on the way in. Please keep your seatbelts fastened until we land.'

Jim had picked up the beacon some 50 miles out, identified it against the special code and, apart from the weather, the landing looked as if it would be perfect – sink rate, air speed...

'Red 47 to control,' he heard Jim breaking radio silence and, immediately, the landing lights came on as Jim continued, 'experiencing engine difficulty, request emergency procedures. Over.'

'Roger, 47, standing by and good luck. Out.'

It was difficult to keep the plane straight while he made his final approach. As each fresh gust of wind caught the port wing, the plane yawed slightly off line. Soon he was over the airport perimeter, coming in. A heavier gust caught the plane just then. Two seconds. He had two seconds to decide whether to abort the landing and go around again.

If he went round, they would be sitting ducks for any MiGs that might be about and number two was starting to heat up. He snapped: 'We're going in.'

His thoughts were racing now. Peculiar runway lights ... irregular, anything that was available, probably. Get it down early, with plenty of runway ... slow it gently. Two's packed up. Shut it off. Close now ...steady, steady ... As the plane neared the runway, another heavier gust hit it, throwing it further to starboard and forcing it down. Wrestling the controls, he realised he was too low, couldn't reach the runway. The irregular lights had momentarily confused him. When the plane touched, just ten metres short of the runway, the left wheel buckled and the plane somersaulted.

For what seemed an age he sat there, helpless, as the plane skidded some 200 metres upside down before it stopped. The smell of fuel. That damn number two. Good God, it's alight...

When the crew opened the emergency door, Igbo ground staff rushed into the upturned aircraft to assist the two passengers, who were suspended upside down, trapped in their seats. Once they were clear, the ground staff saved more than half of the cargo before the flames became too much.

The following day a Nigerian bomb destroyed what was left of the aircraft.

The subsequent investigation referred to all the possible causes: the weather; the faulty or damaged port inner engine; the runway lights; the threat of enemy action; the pilot's snap decision.

Should Bill have gone round again? If he had done so, a MiG might have got them all – pilot and crew, passengers, plane and medical supplies. Who could tell? Bill had about two seconds to make his decision.

Most of us felt he got it right. We blamed the war and thanked God that neither Bill nor anyone else was hurt.

Fintan and Jane could joke as much as they liked about their 'topsy-turvy arrival in Biafra'. At least, they could joke about it.

The last flight to Port Harcourt before it was captured was my most dangerous experience. Fighting was quite near the airport when I received an urgent note from Doctor Lucy O'Brien. Lucy was a missionary sister who was medical officer-in-charge of the Caritas Medical Programme in Biafra. 'We are simply desperate. It was never worse. No drugs, no bandages, no cotton wool, no syringes. Our hospital floor is covered with dying people. Tony, try to get us some supplies as soon as possible. Lucy.'

I asked many pilots to fly, but they felt it was too dangerous. Eventually a Portuguese pilot, Captain João Reis, came to my office.

'Tony, I'm ready to risk it. Will you fly with me?'

'Of course. Do you think we can make it, João?'

'If we do a spiral landing it'll be OK.'

I had no idea what he meant by 'a spiral landing' and somehow I felt sure it would be better for my nerves if he didn't explain it. I'd know soon enough. It was dark when we took off from São Tomé, no moonlight, a beautiful night for our purpose. Sitting in the cockpit with João as we approached the Biafran coast, the distant shellfire seemed innocent, like shooting stars low on the horizon. As we got closer, the scale of the bombardment became apparent. I had seen anti-aircraft fire, 'flak', many times, but never anything like this. The intensity of the bombardment was beyond my comprehension. It seemed impossible that anyone could survive down there.

We saw very heavy fighting some miles from the airport. João studied it for a moment. The responsibility for the decision to continue, or turn back, was his alone. He didn't mince his words: 'Meu Deus! Tony, that's heavy fighting down there. We'll get closer to the airport before we start the spiral. It'll reduce the danger a bit. Keep cool and keep praying. OK. Here we go!'

The spiral landing was far from a pleasant experience. It was like being in a cake-mixer, turning around in circles. Those circles seemed to get tighter and tighter as we descended. At the last moment, it seemed, João turned the aircraft into the wind, slammed on the power on all four engines, abruptly cutting what he called our 'sink rate'. Almost immediately, he dropped the power again and we landed with a tremendous thump.

As soon as the doors of the aircraft were open, Finbarr Horrigan came on board, looking tense and nervous: 'Welcome, lads, but for God's sake keep those engines running. The Nigerians are only a half mile up the road. Let's get the boxes on the trucks and get the hell out of here!'

João and I tossed out the boxes of medicine, kicking some off, throwing others. Finbarr and his co-workers hastily grabbed them and their lorries were already driving away up side roads as we closed the doors.

As I locked the doors, João had the plane taxiing into position and I was scarcely in my seat when he took off. The plane seemed to climb almost vertically but I didn't care. It was enough that we were climbing, heading for the friendly sky and away from that hell-on-earth bombardment.

An hour later, we landed at São Tomé. The fall of Port Harcourt had been announced while we were on our way back.

* * *

Soon after the capture of Port Harcourt, other strategic towns were captured by the Nigerians. At Calabar and the nearby smaller towns of Ikang and Ikot Ene, Biafran troops fiercely resisted the 'invaders' but they could not hold out against the military might of the Nigerian army. Each battle brought great loss of life and terrible injuries of every nature.

Had Major Okpara survived the big battle at Calabar? When the area around Oron fell, what had happened to Captain Ejiofor and Des Perry and the good 'mama' who had all contributed to saving my skin?

At the Ikot Ene hospital, Sr Mary and her community were fortunate to evacuate shortly before the bombardment of the town started. Their patients and staff went with them. Had Ahaji, Idigo and the other soldiers who arrested me got away too – or had they been lost at nearby Ikang?

* * *

Many people thought that Biafra would surrender when Port Harcourt fell. They were wrong. The loss of the airport was a major blow to the Biafrans but they quickly converted the road at Uli town into an airstrip.

The new airstrip was only twenty-one metres wide, compared to a normal runway which would have a minimum of forty-five metres. There was no instrument landing system and pilots depended on the help of unrecorded radio beacons, some of them mobile.

In an effort to close it down, the Nigerian MiGs and Ilyushins strafed and bombed it during the day. As each day ended, the Biafrans filled in the craters again before the JCA aircraft arrived during the night.

The 'Intruder' attacked Uli airstrip at night. Every night, the bomber stayed at a safe, high altitude. From there, he tracked the first JCA aircraft and tried to bomb it on landing. He usually carried between four and eight bombs but had limited fuel capacity. Colonel Wickman, then director of technical affairs of the airlift, devised a plan with the pilots to address the problem.

Captain Tony Johnsonn, who had combat experience, normally took the first flight. With plenty of fuel and a minimal cargo, he maintained a holding position over Uli. As Johnsonn circled the airstrip, he appealed to the captain of the Nigerian bomber: 'Calling Nigerian aircraft over Uli. This is the captain of the church relief flight about to land at Uli. I'm carrying baby food only. Please allow me to land without striking. Over.'

'Roger, church pilot. Land there, baby, and I'll blow you out of existence. Over and out.'

Johnsonn then radioed the control room to request the landing lights. As soon as the lights came on, he made a normal
approach and switched on the aircraft lights at the usual distance. Instead of landing, though, he flew down the airstrip
at about fifty feet. About half-way, he put on power, switched
off his lights and climbed quickly back to a high altitude. As
he doused his lights, the landing lights were also switched
off.

The Nigerian bomber followed him but stayed high to
avoid the Biafran anti-aircraft guns. Each time, he dropped
one or two bombs in the vague hope of hitting Johnsonn's
aircraft or getting a 'near miss'. Because of his altitude, the
'Intruder's bombing was often wildly inaccurate.

Johnsonn repeated the procedure several times until the
'Intruder' ran out of either fuel or bombs. Then the JCA
flights landed one after the other, their heavy loads compensat-
ing for Johnsonn's light one.

On one of his off-duty nights, Captain Johnsonn and his
crew were replaced by Captain Klepp, first officer Markant
and flight engineer Hough. They had two passengers on
board, Fr Dick Kissane and Br Walter Maccagno. I saw them
off at the airport and wished them well.

When I returned to the office some time afterwards, Annie
Walsh, one of my co-workers, looked worried:

'Everything OK, Annie?'

'I'm afraid not, Tony. This arrived from the control tower
at the airport.'

As I took the message I had a sense of foreboding.
Reluctantly, I read: 'Regret to announce a direct hit at Uli
airstrip by 'Intruder' on Captain Klepp's aircraft. Will keep
you informed. Commanding Officer, Uli Airport.'

I decided to fly on the second JCA flight to find out what
happened. As we approached the airstrip, we saw the
'Intruder' returning to Nigeria. When we landed, I could
smell what I thought was burning human flesh and got
ready to hear the worst. As we approached the bombed air-

craft, we could see one of its wings burnt to a cinder and the other lying on the tarmac. A young Biafran had found an intact fuel tank in the wing and was draining the last drops of fuel from it into a petrol tin. I asked him:

'My friend, were they all killed?'

There was puzzlement in his voice:

'Oh, Father, you know God would never let them be killed. They're in hospital for small treatment.

At Ihiala hospital, Sr Thecla reassured me more: 'Oh yes, Tony, they'll be fine. They had some burns but they're recovering now. I'll take you to them.'

Minutes later, I was greeting Dick, Walter and Bill Hough, my relief all too obvious. I asked Dick what had happened.

'Well, the flight was uneventful, Tony, all the way from São Tomé until we were grinding to a halt here at the airstrip. Suddenly, there was a burst of fire under the cockpit, on the right wing, and at the rear of the plane. It seems the 'Intruder' had scored an oblique hit with a bomb on the runway some 80 yards from where we were about to park. Bill, here, took charge at our end.'

Propped up in the next bed, Bill looked embarrassed as Dick continued, extolling his heroism. When the fire started, Bill had burst open the door from the cockpit to get to them. Together, they had scrambled over 'a mountain of stockfish' to get to a rear door. When Bill forced open the door, he tied a rope to a stanchion and the three of them, in turn, swung out from the plane, clear of the flames and safely negotiating the drop of fifteen feet. The vacuum created by the flames was sucking them back, forcing them to crawl on their hands and knees to get clear. The melting tar on the airstrip got on to their shoes and clothes, causing their burns, but fortunately, they were sufficiently clear to avoid catching fire.

They could only stare helplessly as much of the aircraft reduced to cinders. Finally, she broke in two and the last of the engines exploded. For twenty minutes, all their attention had been focused on that incandescent ball of fire.

While this was happening, Aumund Klepp and Bill Markant had made their escape from the cockpit window, on the other side of the aircraft. The two groups had watched the plane burn itself out, unaware that the others had survived. Bill and Dick had even enlisted Des McGlade's help to secure some souvenirs for the pilots' families! As the flames eased off, the two pilots decided to walk around their plane for a last look. When they came round the aircraft, they were like ghostly apparitions to the others!

As Dick said: 'The sense of relief was far headier than any whiskey... but there's been something of a party atmosphere since! Y'see, Tony, the sisters did a great job in making us somewhat respectable looking again and they started our treatment with just the right spirit. After all, the Doctor ordered us to rest,' he winked at Bill, 'with plenty of sedation.'

The JCA pilots were a very special group of people. It was amazing how well they all blended in together, forming a tight-knit team – 'the Squadron', as Mac and Nicholai sometimes referred to it. Whether they were there for two weeks or two years, everyone belonged in the camaraderie which included everyone who helped the airlift, either in São Tomé or Uli.

'Mac', Captain John McCommie, was one of the most popular JCA pilots. He, and some others, gave generously of their free time – and their earnings – to the children's hospital. Most of the pilots were very highly motivated, determined to do whatever they could to ease the children's suffering.

For the younger pilots, Mac was the mentor, the 'old hand' who knew all the ropes. One of the most common questions they asked was about kwashiorkor. They had all seen the photographs of 'the starving children' but lifting a real child on to a plane seemed different. The condition looked worse at close quarters than any photograph could depict it but, on the other hand, the sense of personal contact and identity with another human being overcame any feelings of squeamishness.

Mac spoke to me about the problem:

'Tony, most of the lads would like to understand this kwashiorkor better. It might make a difference when we're flying the children from Uli to the hospital. Maybe there's a way we could make the journey easier for the kids and most of us would like to be able to explain it to friends at home.'

'I agree, Mac, I'm often asked about kwashiorkor, too. We need to work out some simple answers in non-medical terms that help people to understand it practically. I'm sure Sr Carmel at the hospital would help us, if we wanted to work up a sheet of answers for typical questions.'

It was quickly arranged. On the agreed morning, Carmel met me at reception: 'Tony, there's something I think you'd really like to see ...'

I had no idea what to expect as she led me, gently but firmly, to St Anthony's Ward. There were a few sisters and nurses gathered outside, looking through the observation panels as we approached – and gales of laughter coming from the children inside. St Anthony's was the ward for children well on their way to recovery. Mac was in fine fettle in the ward! As he went through his repertoire of magic tricks and songs, it seemed as if we were just as enthralled as the children in the ward. These children had never heard of Rolf Harris, but they certainly knew his 'didgeridoo' now.

As always with children, what they enjoyed most were the things that they could attempt themselves. Mac did a very simple trick with his right hand, making it appear like an ostrich head. Then he talked to his ostrich 'friend' and moved his thumb to help his 'friend' talk back. Carmel told me that every time Mac did this trick – or a variant of it – the children spent the next few days busily talking to their new 'friends' in every corner of the hospital.

When Mac finished his last song with the children, we got down to business. Anyone who asked about kwashiorkor should be given a single page hand-out which described the disease in non-medical language and answered the most common questions. If it took more than a minute to read, it was too long!

Medical notes were quickly edited down to the essentials. Then Carmel read the draft, emphasising the key words, while Mac timed her:

'Kwashiorkor is a Ga word ... normally rare ... only when child is weaned too abruptly ... Human beings adapt to most foods ... but children take longer ... don't yet have these abilities ... need a gentle transition after weaning ... cause is lack of protein rather than a lack of food ...'

'First sign is often diarrhoea ... the liver ... the puffy eyes ... the hair changes colour ... the child is weak ... crying incessantly ... brain damage is a danger ... provide them with proteins ... a small proportion need intensive care.'

'Happily, with good food and good care, most recover fully.'

'Well... How long did it take, Mac?'

'One minute, seven seconds – just the job. Just as well! I'd better be on my way to bed. I'm flying this evening.'

Mac and I left the hospital, together. As we drove, he turned to me: 'It seems all we can do is get them here for the doctors to work on.'

'I wouldn't say "all", Mac, and neither would anyone else...'

'Tony, I don't mean it like that, but the whole situation is getting to most of the pilots. The flak seems to be getting worse, more of it and better directed. Some of the younger lads are thinking of pulling out, going home. I can understand that, particularly with their frustration at how little we seem to be achieving. It just gets us down.'

'Each of us can only do so much, Mac. What you pilots do saves thousands of lives every day. You know that.'

'Yes, I know that all right but it just gets to us that it never seems to be enough. I'm here for the duration of the war, anyhow. Look, Tony, I want you to know that, no matter how bad the flak is, I will fly as long as there is someone to crew for me. Sorry for sounding off, but it just had to come out.'

'I wish I could say something better than thanks, Mac, but thank you, anyhow. You know you're always welcome to sound off or anything else you want, with me. You'd better get some sleep.'

As he got out of the car, he grinned:

'Thanks yourself, we'll talk more later.'

That night São Tomé was busy with the JCA flights. Each crew flew two flights to Biafra. Mac's first flight was scheduled for 6.10 pm, with Richard Holzman, Heinz Raab and Arthur Thompson. They had a cargo of baby food, medicines, salt and stockfish. The four wives of the crew were at the airport to see Mac's flight take off. He waved at us as he moved the aircraft slowly down the runway before take-off. Bright moonlight illuminated the aircraft as it gained altitude. It was a beautiful night, far from ideal for clandestine flying.

The estimated time for Mac's return to São Tomé was 9.35 pm but flights were often delayed due to off-loading problems at Uli. The 'Intruder' caused many more delays. No one was particularly worried when Mac's aircraft didn't return on time. I met Larry Raab returning from his second flight: 'Larry, you left thirty-five minutes after Mac. How come he's not back?'

'I don't know. I didn't see him at Uli. It was very busy there tonight with both JCA and Red Cross flights. Sorry, Tony, he could have been there. I just didn't see him.'

The wives of the crew were becoming anxious. I tried to calm them: 'Technical problems often need attention at Uli. So why don't you get a drink or something to eat in the bar while we wait for the flight to return.'

Captain Michael Sherry's flight was the last to return. I asked if he had noticed anything unusual.

'Not really, Tony. What's up?'

'Mac hasn't been back all night.'

'That's not too good... Look Tony, on my second flight to Uli, I saw a fire burning beyond the Port Harcourt area. I thought it was a bush fire and didn't bother about it... I still think it was a bush fire but it should be checked. I'll do that. I can be airborne in about ten minutes.'

'No, Michael. I think we should stick to the search plan.'

'You're right, Tony. I'll mark the position on a chart. It's just...'

'I know, Michael. We all feel that way about Mac.'

I asked the crews to search for Mac's aircraft. They were all willing to take off again and search for the missing plane, so we put into effect the JCA search plan which co-ordinated such searches in a carefully structured way. The governor was informed and he instructed two Portuguese light aircraft to join in the search. As an additional precaution, the sea search was supported by the JCA ocean-going motor launch.

I flew on the first aircraft with Larry Raab. It was bright daylight as we arrived over the Port Harcourt area. We were dangerously close to the city when Fr Tom Cunningham radioed a recall to all pilots. As soon as we landed in São Tomé, Tom came on board looking very strained:

'Mac's wrecked aircraft has been found near the Biafran frontier. There are no survivors.'

By this time the wives were beginning to suspect the worst. I asked them to return to their hotel and I would let them know as soon as we heard some definite news. As soon as we confirmed the news, Sr Audrey and two nurses from the children's hospital came with me to tell the wives.

A chartered Boeing aircraft from Martinair, a Dutch airline, brought a large consignment of relief supplies to São Tomé. The captain agreed to fly some church pilots and relief workers back on his return flight to Amsterdam. I was at the airport to see them off. As the aircraft was leaving, I noticed Gary Libbus, a load-master who worked for the Canadian Presbyterian organisation, Canairelief. He was normally such a very jolly person that I was surprised to see tears running down his face. I put my hand on his shoulder:

'Gary, let's go and have a drink.' We sat in a quiet corner of the lounge. 'What about a brandy?'

'Get me a whiskey, please.' He wiped tears from his eyes.

'Gary, would you like to share with me what's upsetting you? Don't feel you have to, but if it helps, please feel free. I'm not in any hurry.'

'Y'see Tony, Gladys and our two sons have left Canada to meet me in Amsterdam. I had planned to fly on that Martinair Boeing and have a holiday with them in Europe. God, they'll be very disappointed to find that I am not on the flight. They haven't had a good holiday in years.'

I waited for a while in silence but then felt it would help him to talk: 'Would you like to tell me why you didn't fly, Gary?'

The tears returned and he found it difficult to talk. I tried to console him: 'Take it easy, Gary. I know this is difficult for you.'

He took a deep breath: 'Good God, Tony, don't you see. It's getting to all of us. We do what we can, yet it never seems to be enough. It gets to us that so many kids are dying in Biafra... Anyway, my boss has asked me to fly tonight. He needs a load-master urgently because one of our lads has fever.'

I was deeply touched. 'Gosh, that's very generous, Gary. You're making a tremendous sacrifice.'

'Ah, sure, it's nothing for me but it's tough on Gladys and the kids. Anyway, I've sent a message to them that I'll get the second Martinair flight, the day after tomorrow.'

Gary flew that night with Donald Merriam, Vincent Wakeling and Raymond Levesque. The clouds were unusually low – ideal conditions for the flights, I thought, as I waved them goodbye.

Later that night, Altino Coelho phoned me from the São Tomé airport control tower. His nervous voice told me there was trouble: 'I'm sorry, Tony. I've just received a message from Uli that Captain Merriam's aircraft crashed on its final approach. It looks as if there are no survivors.'

For a while, I hoped against hope. He had only said 'it looks'. When the confirmation came, I was devastated thinking of Gladys and the two boys, waiting in vain in Amsterdam.

The statisticians and the strategists could pontificate all they
liked about how low our losses were, in relative terms. They
weren't statistics to us, but real friends, warm human beings.
Apart from the incidents involving Mac and Gary, there were
seven other fatal ones involving JCA aircraft. Shot down or
crashed, the difference was often a minute technicality, always academic.

One hundred and twenty-two Biafran and thirty-five
North American and European JCA workers, including seventeen pilots, sacrificed their lives during the relief programme.

Mac and the others were right. The airlift would have
needed an air force to do the job that was needed to be done.
We had a maximum of sixteen planes at any one time – just a
squadron, as Mac said, with a fierce pride. The squadron was
suffering its casualties. It had never fired a shot – and never
would. Its battle honours were different, to be measured in
lives saved, tons of food and medicine flown, happy children's faces. They wouldn't have any medals or stone monu-
ments – but the memory of them would be etched in the
hearts and minds of many children like Moses Meze and
Lucy Eke. That was an epitaph worth having.

The 5,500 clandestine sorties flown would be a proud record
for any squadron. Even a squadron with the full resources of
a major power – money, logistics, and fully co-ordinated
equipment – would rightly regard it as a great achievement.

This squadron had to make do with what was available
through sponsorship and the wonderful, but fluctuating,
generosity of donors. For a group of people who had come
together on an *ad hoc*, largely voluntary basis, the achievement of maintaining the airlift over almost two years was
astonishing.

Amassing over 60,000 tonnes of food and medicine at São
Tomé, mainly through voluntary donations, was an extraordinary achievement. Flying them into a war zone was, at
that time, unprecedented for a voluntary organisation. The

airlift enabled the emergency centres to feed four million peo-
ple daily, saving more than a million lives – mostly children's.
Joint Church Aid had every right to be proud of the pilots.
In turn, they took a jaunty pride in JCA.

Many people at Uli had painful reasons to remember Guy
Fawkes night in 1968. Three bombs landed near the airstrip at
11 pm, four more hit at 1 am. Rocket and strafing attacks were
reported. Some ammunition exploded and there were other,
less reliable, reports of unidentified explosions.

Uli was Biafra's main air link to the outside world. The
Biafran military used it to fly in ammunition and other military supplies. The churches and the Red Cross used it at the
same time to fly in relief supplies of food and medicines.
There wasn't any other way but it made it easy for the propagandists to accuse the churches of carrying weapons.

A small amount of ammunition had been left near the
airstrip, in error, by the military earlier in the evening.
Nobody knew quite why it exploded, but it added to the general confusion at the time the four bombs fell. The Intruder's
first three bombs had fallen harmlessly a distance away and
everyone hoped that this second lot would be no closer.

Glade had just greeted Captain Kjell Erik Bäckström.

'Good to see you, Captain. What have you got for us?'

'Hi, Glade. Five and a half tonnes of salt, three of rice, two
maize and I've got some surgical gloves, needles and clamps
in the cockpit.'

'Oh boy, Kjell. You'll be popular.'

The ground crews had the doors open and were already
starting to unload as Glade jumped out of the plane, yelling:

'C'mon lads, let's keep it moving.'

Then the Intruder's last four bombs landed. When Glade
came to, about twenty yards away, there seemed to be bodies
everywhere. As others came to help, they found Glade
administering the Last Rites to the dying and badly injured.
Lorries were pressed into service as temporary ambulances

to take the injured and the dead to Ihiala hospital. By morning, there were twelve dead and twenty eight had been injured – including Bäckström, his co-pilot Ölsen and Glade himself. Ölsen's lower leg was badly shattered and needed major surgical work in Europe to save it.

Glade had multiple shrapnel injuries, some of which he carried until the war was over. One had gone through the calf of his leg, another had struck him behind the ear, much too close for comfort. There was more in his hips, his abdomen and his right arm. Some the doctors removed, more had to be left until a better opportunity.

It irritated Des that he had to use his left hand to shake hands for a long time afterwards. At least the other wounds didn't show, didn't need tiresome explanations.

Bäckström had got a nasty blow to his back and his legs were badly cut by flying fragments. As soon as they had bandaged his legs, however, he insisted on returning to the airstrip. His engineer had stayed with the plane and had helped organise the rest of the unloading. After that, he had identified over 150 holes in the DC 7's exterior and serious damage to the starboard outboard engine.

Bäckström arrived back:

'Can she fly, Max?'

'Risky, Captain. The other three engines are OK, and I haven't found any vital damage, but she's really badly shot up. Nobody could be sure without a full investigation. She's fully unloaded though. The three engines should be enough while she's empty. I'd be willing to chance it.'

'No Max. I'll take it on my own. I appreciate the offer but it only needs a pilot to get it back. Let's have no unnecessary risks. Is she ready?'

'As ready as she can be. Good luck, Kjell.'

Within minutes, Bäckström was airborne. Number four was rough but gave him enough power to climb quickly away from Uli. As soon as he was clear, he shut it down and made it safely back to São Tomé on three engines. The DC 7 was so badly damaged that it could never be used again but it was an invaluable source of precious spares at São Tomé.

A week later, with his legs still bandaged, Bäckström insisted on returning to normal flying duties.

Most of the fighting was on the ground, fought between two groups of men, and sometimes women, who knew and understood each other too well. We were often proud of the generosity of people in Europe and America in supporting the airlift relief programmes but it was from Europe and America that the killing machines came, too. The war was fought with Northern weapons, ammunition and mercenaries. Much of the training was European or European-inspired. Yet it was an African war where both sides accepted only what they felt suited them from the European power brokers.

The Biafran troops generally had the worst of it. These inexperienced soldiers, some as young as fifteen, many of them conscripts, were sent to the front line after two weeks of training. They were often controlled by army officers who stayed a safe distance away from the firing line. Food and military supplies were usually inadequate. Medical back-up, air coverage and radio communications were almost non-existent.

The Nigerian army was better off. There was a substantial supply line, medical attention for wounded soldiers readily available, sophisticated radio communication, a professional training programme for recruits. They had qualified local and expatriate military strategists and advisers. But the people were the same.

Sadly this war pitted brother against brother. They were African brothers, though, who once lived peacefully together, and now fought their war in an African way, with a distinctly African perception of honour and chivalry. Despite their determination to kill each other, traditional courtesies were extended and adapted to the strange circumstances.

Fr Matty Murphy tells how the Biafran soldiers managed matters when he arrived to hear confessions. Bullets would be flying as he arrived but then one of the soldiers would shout to the Nigerian soldiers in their dug-outs:

'Are you there, my brothers? Can you hear me?'

'Yes,' a few Nigerian soldiers would reply in unison.

'I beg you, don't shoot for fifteen minutes, please. Our Reverend Father is here to hear our confessions. So give chance now.'

'OK. We won't shoot.'

Tolerance took precedence and the unofficial cease-fire held for the fifteen minutes while Matty gave spiritual comfort to the young soldiers. Similar unofficial cease-fire periods were arranged when the soldiers wanted to bathe in a river or stream. The terms were always strictly honoured. African courtesies were observed in an unwritten code of chivalry as strict and as time-honoured as the one that Europe sadly seemed to have forgotten.

Christian Aid and the Catholic Fund for Overseas Development, two London-based charities, sent a consignment of relief supplies to São Tomé. The carrier was a British-based cargo company.

While the aircraft was being unloaded, Captain Gerry Healy invited me to the bar for a drink. Boyish-looking, with fluffy red hair and blue eyes, he spoke of his Irish ancestry. It was well after lunch and the bar was almost empty. Siesta time was sacred for most people in São Tomé.

After a short silence, he said: 'You know, Tony, I really could do with a break just now. I'm spaced out. I was looking forward to a few days on this paradise island, doing nothing except soaking in the sun on a beach and listening to the sound of the waves breaking on the shore. But I'm not sure.'

'But why, Gerry? A few days here would do you good.'

He looked around the bar. We were alone.

'Damn it, that boss of mine is most unreasonable. He told me to get back to London as soon as possible because there's something urgent on the cards.'

'Urgent? Sounds interesting. Or is it?'

'Well, that's what I really want to talk to you about. I don't feel good with what I am doing and I don't know how the hell I ever got into this business.'

'Would you like to talk about it?'

He smiled, and breathed heavily: 'It doesn't make sense. We've flown here with food and medicines for Biafrans. Now we've to fly back to London as soon as we can to carry a cargo of bombs – to prevent the same relief supplies landing at Uli. Tony, can you imagine how I feel when I see the poor Biafran kids on television? I feel like throwing up. Most of the pilots flying to Nigeria feel the same. Many of us talk about it when we meet.'

'As far as my boss is concerned, we simply deliver freight for anyone who pays us. As the boss puts it, we're "glorified delivery boys". Relief today, bombs tomorrow, electric parts the following day for whoever pays the wages. We're not supposed to notice, or have feelings.'

I felt sorry for Gerry. I could see he was really upset.

'I don't understand. Why does your boss want the cargo to Lagos in such a hurry?'

'It seems they've run out of bombs. The same thing is always happening in Lagos. Nigerians don't seem to worry about supplies until the last of the supplies has actually gone. No matter how often they're told, they won't plan their requirements in time.'

'I flew a consignment to Lagos a few weeks ago and met a group of pilots over a drink. Many of them were disgusted at the attacks on the relief planes. Feelings were running high with some feeling it was making war on babies.' He looked around the bar again, before continuing: 'A few of us got together afterwards and agreed that a little delivery man's gossip might be in order.'

He winked at me. For a moment I was worried.

'Gerry, you know I can't...'

'No, no, Tony, this is just something we want to do for the

kids. None of us give a damn about our bosses really – they
make a fortune out of the whole business. But we need to be
sure that any gossip we pass on is used discreetly so that it
will do some good without unnecessarily risking our necks in
Lagos.'

'That I can surely promise, Gerry, but what gossip?'

'The lads in Lagos regularly meet up with an Egyptian
pilot who bombs Uli. His complaints that the Nigerian Air
Force has no idea of logistics confirm what we know of them
running out of bombs. He said that on several occasions he
was ordered to take off from Lagos without bombs just to
cause confusion at Uli. If he's there tonight, you can be pretty
sure he has no bombs. Would that make much of a difference?'

'A big difference, Gerry, and thank you but it would mean
a lot more if we knew the day before so that we could use it to
plan. That way we could get not just more goods in but salt
and other awkward loads could be flown in with relative
ease. Even one such night would be precious.'

'Let me see what we can do, Tony. There's a slight fault
with our port outer blade. Maybe we can be a bit fussy. After
all, delivery boys shouldn't risk their lives, now should they?'

He grinned mischievously.

'I can understand why you need a break here in São Tomé,
Gerry. All this must be very stressful for you.'

'Look, Tony, we needed to know that whatever we did
would be useful. We can't do it often, but we'll be glad to do
what we can. Old Perky, my flight engineer, understands, so
let's just wait for him. Drink up, let's have another.' As Gerry
was ordering, the engineer arrived.

'Tony, meet Perky, the best flight engineer in the business.
Nobody but his mother ever called him George Perkins!'

'Gerry, we're in trouble. Oh yes, a Scotch if you don't mind,
Guv, but I don't like the look of that blade. Dodgy that... yes
dodgy.'

For the next couple of minutes they went through a well-
rehearsed pantomime act of mock-serious discussion about

the propeller blade, emphasised with great sucking of teeth
and groans:

'Risky ... could lose the plane ... your responsibility ...
couldn't be sure ... only a new blade would really do ... but
on the other hand ... important contract ... wouldn't like to let
the boss down ... but safety all-important ... shouldn't risk
the plane unnecessarily ... my responsibility ... don't really
know ... very risky.'

'How long do you think, Perky?'

'If we report every four hours or so, we could swing it out
till the morning after tomorrow. If we tell Clarke that we
'hope' to have it fixed tomorrow, it should work.'

'I agree. You might have gathered, Tony, that Clarke's our
boss. He won't release the contract or recall one of the other
aircraft, if he thinks it might be fixed tomorrow. He's well able
to stall the Nigerians, too.'

'Let me see. If we leave on Wednesday morning at, say 4 am,
and fly with minimum stops to Britain and back to Lagos, the
earliest we could possibly be back there would be about 6 pm
Thursday. That would be breaking a lot of rules – which, of
course we would generously offer to do, to impress both
Clarke and the Nigerians. That would leave you safe from the
bomber for tonight, Tuesday and Wednesday. How's that?'

'Fantastic, Gerry, but are you taking too much of a risk?
And can we be certain that they won't get the bombs some
other way?'

'No risk, really, so long as nobody talks, Tony. At least,
talking to a priest, we know that you've some practice at
keeping secrets!'

'Clarke is very predictable, too. You can be absolutely certain that if the Nigerians take the shipment off him or he has
to recall another plane, he'll be so mad that he'll be fuming
down the phone at us almost as soon as he knows. He would
simply have to vent his frustration. Right, Perky?'

'Oh yes, you can rely on that.'

'Right, Tony, that's settled, then. Any hint from Clarke of a change in plan and I'll let you know immediately but nobody else hears about this little chat. It wouldn't do if we got a reputation as gossips.'

'I really don't know how to thank you both.'

'As soon as we've finished doing our "party piece" on the telephone for Clarke's benefit, you can point us towards the best beach...'

'With the biggest and best stocked bar,' Perky added.

'Don't worry, lads, I know the best one and I'd be glad to drive you. There's a good bar not too far from it. I'll even buy a few rounds.'

Gerry became quite serious again. He looked at Perky, who nodded almost imperceptibly: 'Tony, this is something we really want to do. Accepting even a drink might spoil it. Just point us to the beach. You get on and make the most of the relevant gossip. We hope it helps.

Maybe the age of European chivalry wasn't quite dead either.

There was a smile on my face as I left the airport in great haste with the good news. I called to the Hotel Jerónimos to see if any of the crews had surfaced from siesta. Captain Rolf Nicholai was in the lounge.

He was surprised to see me: 'Any trouble, Tony?'

'No, eh...Rolf, please don't ask me my source, but I want to tell you that I'm satisfied that the 'Intruder' won't have bombs on board for the next few nights. Let's get the word around to the lads that we can rely on tonight, Tuesday and Wednesday nights. After that, he'll have his supplies again and will probably be keen to make up for lost time.'

'Are you sure, Tony?'

'Trust me, Rolf, I'm quite sure. Three nights, starting tonight. How do you think we could use them best?'

'It's a bit late to change anything for tonight. Maybe it will help the lads to make the third run. We can try to shift as much of the straightforward stuff as possible tonight. If we start now, we can have "Operation Salt" mounted for tomorrow

night and, on Wednesday night, we should be able to clear practically everything we have here. Tony, are you really sure?'

'My friend, it's a long time since I've felt so sure of any
information.'

As I left the Jerónimos, Rolf was shouting for the other
pilots. It would be a hectic few days but they would make the
most of it. Salt was always an awkward load, heavy and slow
to unload, leaving the aircraft a sitting target for too long.
'Operation Salt' had been planned more as a theoretical exer-
cise than in any real hope that an opportunity like this would
arise.

By Thursday morning we had delivered a record tonnage
of supplies to Uli, including well over a hundred tonnes of the
precious salt.

It was long after midnight on Thursday night when the
'Intruder' dropped his next bombs on a relatively quiet Uli
airstrip. It was as if he suspected what had happened and just
wanted to tell us he was back in business.

* * *

My reminiscing about the JCA flights was interrupted when
one of the Alitalia hostesses wheeled up a duty-free trolley.
The contrast between the amazing choice of luxuries on offer
and the lifestyle of my friends was stark. Back in Biafra, a loaf
of fresh bread could be a luxury.

At Fiumicino airport, an Alitalia bus took us to the arrivals
area where the formalities were perfunctory and fast. I was
soon outside, greeting Bayer who had come to the airport to
meet me.

CHAPTER 8

Guilty, but Insane

As soon as we greeted each other, Bayer drove me straight to the Vatican. He told me that he had asked for an appointment with Archbishop Benelli. Apart from that, he insisted on keeping the conversation light and informal until he parked the car in the Vatican grounds. Then his voice became stern:

'Look, Tony, I feel I should warn you. This won't be easy. Benelli is convinced that we shouldn't use those parachutes for an airdrop. He feels they are quasi-military equipment. Even the good Lord himself might find it difficult to change his mind. So be prepared for a disappointment.'

'C'mon, Carlo. We've nothing to lose.'

When we asked to see Benelli, an official in Vatican uniform phoned the Secretariat of State. The reply didn't take long:

'Sorry, Monsignori, His Excellency Archbishop Benelli is not available, but Monsignori Casseroli and Gallina will be happy to receive you in Room 24 on the second floor.'

As we went on the old-fashioned elevator to the second floor, Bayer put his right hand over his mouth and nudged me:

'You see, Tony. The old tricks. "Not available". What does that mean?'

We entered Room 24 and after a brief delay the two Monsignori joined us. Casseroli spoke for both:

'Welcome! You must be tired, Father Byrne, after the long journey from Biafra. Monsignor Bayer, it's good to see you again.'

I started to make my appeal: 'Monsignori, the Biafran situation is desperate. Uli airport will soon be captured by the

Nigerians. Food and medicines are extremely scarce and the death rate is increasing daily. I've come to...'

With that there was a knock at the door and a nun entered, dressed in a long black habit with a white veil. She looked nervous and walked briskly across the room carrying a note. 'Excuse me. Sorry. Your Excellency, this is for you. It's urgent.' She handed the note to Casseroli, who read it and let the message sink in. He said nothing for a while but blinked a few times. Then he stood up and said apologetically:

'You must excuse us for a few moments.'

He hurriedly walked out of the room, beckoning Gallina to follow him.

'What's going on, Carlo?'

'God only knows, Tony, but it's something urgent. I presume... well perhaps, Benelli is telling them what to say to us!'

The two Monsignori returned to the room after a short time. Casseroli looked at me intently and nodded:

'OK, now we can continue, Father Byrne.'

'Well, as I was saying, the situation in Biafra is very serious and I've come to the Vatican asking you to reconsider your policy about the use of the parachutes. That would allow us to...'

Casseroli lifted his right hand, the open palm towards me.

'Just a moment. Excuse me for interrupting, but I've just received a communiqué from the Nuncio in Lagos. He says Biafra is about to be captured. Ojukwu fled the country yesterday, and is believed to be in the Ivory Coast. I'm afraid it's too late for parachutes. You must try to get relief supplies by road from Nigeria to former Biafra.'

I was shocked at this news and stared at the two men. Gallina broke the silence: 'We must pray that the Nigerian forces will show restraint.'

He eyed his watch, then looked at Bayer:

'We're preparing a speech for the Pope's public address in St Peter's Square tomorrow. It's very important. So I'm sure you'll excuse us and allow us to continue with that work.'

'Could I ask your opinion? The Holy Father wants us to include in his speech a challenge to the Nigerians to avoid genocide. I've implored him not to use the word genocide because it's too sensitive. What do you think?'

Bayer didn't hesitate: 'The Nigerians have always claimed it wasn't a war of genocide. It's good for the Pope to remind them of that and challenge them to prove that they meant what they said.'

Casseroli raised an eyebrow, then, to my surprise, he turned to me: 'And what do you think?'

'Well, I'm not sure, but on balance, I agree with Monsignor Bayer. If the Pope puts the challenge to the Nigerians, I believe they'll be careful to avoid unnecessary bloodshed.'

We bade them farewell and left the Vatican for Bayer's apartment.

As soon as we arrived, Carlo showed me to my room: 'I'll make some coffee in a little while, Tony. I'm sure you'd like a chance to freshen up first.' The emotional impact of the news I'd heard in the Vatican overpowered me and I needed to be alone. As I slumped in a chair, I was glad that Carlo understood, grateful for his sensitivity.

It was over. The reality of the situation hit me. What was the purpose of this useless war? Why did more than one million civilians have to die?

I thought of the real victims of the war, the brain damaged 'combat boys' as they were called in Biafra. These ex-soldiers would have to live miserably for the rest of their lives, roaming the streets, shouting meaningless speeches to themselves. Why should the thousands of blind and maimed former soldiers have to carry the scars of war for the remaining years of their lives? It was difficult to console these young men, many of whom had no legs, lying on beds and on the floors of hospitals in Biafra. Some might get artificial limbs – but not the many who needed them.

But most of all I thought of the children – thousands of

lovely children, each one an individual like Moses or Lucy,
who had to walk on matchstick legs from one refugee camp
to the other. Why did they have to suffer... and die?
I thought of the main actors in the war, too.
Ojukwu was now in safe exile, away from the final onslaught. Gowon was beginning to taste the thrills of victory. I
hoped and prayed that he would try to restrain his conquer-
ing army from unnecessary bloodshed and from creating
total mayhem. Somehow, I felt he was a man who would be
magnanimous in victory and have the vision to promote
reconciliation.

The suppliers of weaponry and those who transported
them would already be lamenting the end of their lucrative
trade. The mercenaries would be telling their war stories to
friends, full of macho fulfilment and financial gain.

The relief pilots might have gained financially but they
need have no doubts about what they had done.

What would happen to the brave missionaries, nuns and
brothers, priests and pastors? Courageous Bishops like
Godfrey Okoye and Joe Whelan and so many other church
personnel had stood beside their people during their agony
and had given all they had to save lives. Now they would
face the Nigerian forces as Biafra fell. Would these church
people be shot? Would the nuns be raped? Or would common
sense and decency prevail, at last?

The knocking on the door got louder. With a start, I realised I
had heard it a few times already.

'Sorry, Carlo, I'll be with you in a minute.'

'Whenever you're ready, Tony. Coffee's ready.'

Some two minutes later, I joined Carlo in the livingroom.
The winter evening gradually turned to dusk and Carlo
switched on some low-powered wall lights. The soft lighting
was gentle on the eyes, relaxing, like the dusk outside. I
found that strange now, having grown accustomed to the
brash light and the vibrant colours with which every evening
in Africa ended so abruptly.

The lighting reflected off the glass on a photograph. Set in a carved wooden frame on the pristine wall of the apartment, the photograph of the young woman smiling somehow seemed striking. The unusual light gave her attractive features a strange air of confidence despite her old-fashioned clothes – a wide-brimmed hat and an ankle-length black coat. I looked inquisitively at Bayer.

He smiled and nodded gently: 'My mother… but I never knew her. She died when I was born.'

'Sorry, Carlo, I didn't know. Had you brothers and sisters?'

'No, unfortunately. I was the only one.'

We lapsed into silence but I felt I had a better understanding of Bayer's complex personality. Again and again, I found my eyes returning to the photograph and contrasting it with Bayer's own face. He shared many of her features, a curious blend which hinted at both compassion and confidence.

Bayer smiled as he watched me compare him with the photograph. There was no hint of embarrassment and his voice was scarcely more than a whisper:

'It's lovely, isn't it? I'm glad you can see some resemblance. Wherever I go, that photo will never be far away.'

* * *

Perhaps it was because of the photograph or maybe that the two nights were full of questions but, one way or another, I can never think of that night in Bayer's apartment in Rome without also remembering a night in Vienna three years later. Bayer had left Caritas Internationalis in 1970 to work in Vienna, helping Eastern European people in the Soviet States.

When I arrived at his apartment, Bayer showed me around, briefly. The only thing I can remember, really, was the photograph, beside a coffee table, as it had been in Rome. We had a few relaxed moments, before Carlo said: 'I felt you wouldn't mind, Tony. I have to "sing for our supper"' – isn't that the expression? The local university has a group of students who are trying to develop an international debating society. When they go to conferences, they need to be able to debate in English if they are to participate fully. Simultaneous translations only cover the formal sessions and, unless their English is good enough, they lose out on the fringe activities.'

'Anyhow, I've agreed to be their guest speaker tonight. I'm to speak on the Biafran conflict for ten minutes and they will sharpen up their skills on me with a question and answer session for perhaps an hour. If you'd like to come, I can promise that you won't be bored.'

'I'd love that, Carlo... I think!'

There was a great buzz of conversation from the fifty or sixty students present in the meeting room. Within minutes, the meeting was called to order and Bayer briefly introduced. He spoke for his allotted ten minutes, emphasising how the war had changed the way people viewed such tragedies:

'The Nigerian civil war was the first war which involved people through regular, up-to-the-minute television reports... people saw what was happening and responded generously ... an airlift that saved lives... the churches working together... felt responsibility to help... tried to broker peace... feed people... a war that acted as a catalyst for change... new aid structures... new thinking.'

As soon as he finished, they got down to the serious business of questioning him, sharpening their English:

'Monsignor, why did the churches get involved in Biafra. It's great that new structures have evolved, but what about the ordinary people, who didn't care about future development? Were they being used? Couldn't governments have done the job better, provided whatever food aid was needed...'

'Or the UN?'

'Wasn't that political interference?'

Bayer smiled at the student. 'There are several good questions there. The churches have considerable moral authority – power if you like. The other side of that is the responsibility that goes with any power. The Christian churches have always sided with the poor, the oppressed, the hungry. We make no

apologies for that. What we do apologise for is that, over the
past 2,000 years, individuals weren't always as Christian as they
should have been, forgetting the churches' true role in their
anxiety to maintain church structures and organisations.

'Sure, governments might have done the job in Biafra, but
that would have been a greater interference, subject to more
suspicion, than the churches' efforts. Many supported the JCA
airlift instead. The consensus needed for a UN operation would
not have been there.'

'But Bayer, surely there's an argument for saying...'

'Hold on, young man, let me finish. I don't believe there's
an argument that you can produce tonight that hasn't been
hotly debated by my colleagues in Rome. None of the decisions
were easy. If we do anything, we're blamed and if we do
nothing, I think we deserve to be blamed. Personally, I always
preferred to be blamed for at least trying to do the right thing.

'If governments had acted, they might have turned the
war into a much bigger conflict. People would have believed
the governments were shipping arms...'

'But, Bayer, they said the churches were...'

'Yes, of course, many propagandists *said* that – but nobody
seriously *believed* it. That was the vital difference. If a national
power was shipping in relief supplies to Biafra, most people
would have been convinced that they were shipping in arms
as well – and for their own motives.'

'On the political question, I'd ask you to consider this.
Would it not have been more political to remain silent and
allow people to die of starvation? Surely such silence could
be interpreted as consent or agreement by the church to what
was going on?

'As far as ordinary Biafrans are concerned, there are more
than a million alive today who would have died but for the
airlift. Many of your brothers and sisters came to São Tomé as
volunteers to build the children's hospital that the Austrian
people donated. Ask them about the suffering they saw...'

'Hold on, Monsignor. My brother was a volunteer in São

Tomé. We know what you mean and none of us are disputing the work done by the churches...'

There were great choruses of assent. Bayer was right that many had friends and relatives who had helped in building the hospital.

'... it's just that we think assumptions should be challenged, before the next tragedy condemns people to repeat mistakes that could be avoided. Isn't it fair to say that the airlift prolonged the suffering by keeping Biafra alive?'

'No, my friends, we did not keep Biafra alive. It's not fair to say that. What we did was to keep innocent people alive in a country they called "Biafra". There's a big difference. Please keep challenging the thinking, though. It's what you do best and it's vital, both to the community and the church.'

'But Bayer, why did you fly over countries illegally? You've no right to break international airspace rules. The end cannot justify the means. You're a radical and the world is destroyed by people like you.'

There were cheers and laughter. Carlo nodded in agreement:

'Sure, I'm a radical... and...You're quite right. Yes, we broke the law. Do you think that laws are there for themselves or to help people? If a fire breaks out in this restaurant this evening, should the fire engines break the speed limits and drive through stop-lights to save our lives?

'Of course the end doesn't justify the means, as such. But there is an issue of proportionality. Laws can't deal with every specific situation. We each have the responsibility to make informed decisions to fit the circumstances – and answer for our actions, if necessary. Let me illustrate that.

'Suppose you're walking home tonight and you see a house on fire, with children in danger inside. Do you have to obtain the permission of the owner before you can enter it to save the children's lives? If you break in to save them, have you broken the law? Are you a radical, if you do?'

There was silence for a moment. Then Bayer pointed at the

students: 'Do you think we should have done nothing, simply observed two thousand children dying every day and not feed them. Are you saying that we should have told these children to say their prayers and sing hymns for peace?'

Loud laughter filled the room, then applause. For an hour more the debate continued. I marvelled at Carlo's patience as the questions gradually became more hackneyed, tiresome repetitions of the barely concealed propaganda that had often passed for news during the war.

A bearded student stood as he put his question in a loud, aggressive tone: 'Bayer, one well known magazine said that the churches financed the war by paying extremely high landing fees in Uli. How can you justify that?'

Bayer laughed loudly: 'So you believe what you read in the papers? What did we say about students challenging assumptions? Good reporters always cross-check their information, but there are many who rely on gossip – "it was reported" – or quasi-official, "leaks" and handouts from "reliable sources".'

'JCA never paid a penny for landing fees in Biafra. I can swear to that. The reporter, or anyone else, could have examined the JCA accounts, certified by one of Europe's most respected firms of chartered accountants. That story was just more propaganda, I'm afraid.'

'Monsignor, can you tell us frankly what was the root cause of this war?'

Bayer hesitated, sipped some water from the glass in front of him: 'Ja, that is the best question of all...

'Rumours had been rampant before and during the war that there would be an international oil crisis. Many said that the world's oil resources were drying up. The former Biafra has copious supplies of oil that is sulphur free. Many people wanted to have access to those supplies.

'The war would never have happened if there were no rich oil wells in the Port Harcourt area. More than a million people died. I'm convinced those people were sacrificed on the altar of oil ... That's the easy part of the answer.'

The students looked shocked but nodded to each other in agreement.

'The more difficult part to explain, my friends, was the role of the colonial and former colonial powers. Everybody knows that colonialism is finished in Africa, but there are many countries who still want to buy their raw materials at the old colonial prices, or less, from their former colonies. These powers are also keen to defend their past behaviour by trying to show that Africans are not mature enough to manage their own affairs. You know the sort of thing...'

There were guffaws of laughter as one student quipped:

'Oh yes, Bayer, we know. We have many lecturers like that!'

Bayer grinned. He was clearly enjoying the lively atmosphere, as he continued with mock severity:

'... as I was saying before my friend interrupted me immaturely, the colonial powers were defending the indefensible...'

'You see, I can't accept that there are colonial countries. I don't know of any country where all the people are colonially minded. It's always just a handful of politicians and power brokers who set out to dominate others. They tend to dominate their own people just as much.

'They have difficulty accepting the new Africa and would like to continue their old dominance, at least economically, by what is beginning to be called "clientelism". Africans will need some time to find the answers that suit themselves, to settle their own internal differences. We should support them, not try to tell them what to do.'

There was applause and cheers before the chairperson called a halt to the proceedings, saying that it was time for supper.

When we sat down in the restaurant, we were soon joined by many other students who had waited in the bar for the debate to finish. There must have been a hundred young men and women sitting on the benches, drinking mainly beer and wine as they waited for the platters of pasta.

Carlo introduced me to many at the table. It surprised me how many of their names he knew, just from university debates. One young woman, a medical student, asked me about the hospital in São Tomé – her brother had been there. When we had exhausted that subject, she became a little personal: 'I'm not sure how I should ask this but were you ever an ordinary priest?'

'You know, I've been asked that question a few times recently. I really must work out a proper answer but I think I know what you mean. Let me tell you about the student group from my first parish in Nigeria. Their leader was a chap called Linus Idika....'

As I told the story of how Linus adapted the play, I had a dozen attentive listeners.They totally identified with Linus' need to get rid of the 'white man stuff' – they had the same problem in adapting the classics. They demanded that I write out the alternative words that Linus had written for 'Santa Lucia' – as nearly as I could remember them. Suddenly, my demure medical student friend was on her feet, the words in her hand, shouting: 'Right folks, new drinking song! To the air of "Santa Lucia".'

Guitars and a clarinet appeared, as if by magic, and Linus would have been thrilled to hear them sing: 'Wine is better in the belly, than in the calabash.'

Shortly after that, Carlo and I excused ourselves, leaving the evening to the young people. When we got to Bayer's apartment, we sat at a coffee table rather like the one we had used that earlier night in Rome. His mother's photograph caught my eye again. I glanced at the photo and then at Carlo.

He was grinning now:

'Yes! I remember, too. Tell me, are you very tired?'

'No, Carlo, there's a lot I'd love to talk about, if you're willing. Somehow, it's hard to discuss much of what happened with anyone else and there's a lot I'd like to catch up on.'

'I feel the same, Tony. Let's make some coffee, though. I've never known the students to waste good beer-drinking money on such frippery!'

We fixed the coffee together, all the time trading stories about our common friends – whatever we knew of their current roles and whereabouts. Between us, we had heard many glowing, but sketchy, reports of the astonishing range of their activities all over Africa, in Asia, the Americas and Europe. As we sat down again, we were quiet for a while, reflective.

'Nigeria's loss, it seems, was everyone else's gain. I know it was traumatic for them to be deported and Nigeria could ill afford to lose their contribution, but, overall, it might have been the best thing that could have happened.'

'But, Carlo, you can't really mean that!'

On 15 January 1970, three days after the war ended, Bishop Joseph Whelan and fifty-seven other missionaries – sisters, brothers and priests – had been arrested. They had been charged only on two minor counts: entering Nigeria unlawfully and accepting employment without the consent, in writing, of the Chief Federal Immigration Officer. The missionaries spent some time under house arrest and in a detention centre before their trials. On 27 January they were tried and sentenced to six months' imprisonment.

Carlo became more reflective: 'You remember the Pope's appeal, Tony. "On bended knees," he appealed to the Nigerians to avoid genocide. He challenged them to show mercy and love to their African brothers and sisters. By and large, they did, with remarkably few atrocities after such a conflict.'

'As a German, I can assure you that even the most disciplined and well-trained armies are difficult to control in victory. Celebrations are inevitable and understandable, but it is all too easy for them to get out of hand. There are always individuals who lose control and exact some personal revenge.'

He paused for a minute, sipping coffee and lighting a cigarette, clearly remembering something specific.

'Yes, in the circumstances, they were remarkably well behaved. The point is, having thought about it, that I'm convinced that the deportation of the missionaries was an important part of that strategy. It focused blame, unfairly of course, on the outsiders – convenient foreign scapegoats – and enabled the Nigerian nation to bind its wounds, quieten the hawks, reunite its people.'

'Our friends were hurt by being branded as criminals. A short period in jail and deportation for 105 missionaries, though, was a small price to pay to save a major bloodbath. I'm convinced that our friends would willingly have paid that price. Of course, it would be nicer if it was acknowledged.'

'But Carlo, how can you be sure?'

'I'm not. I don't suppose we'll ever be sure, but I'll never forget the "bended knees" speech the Pope made. Our diplomat friends really were on their bended knees to Pope Paul before he spoke, imploring him not to use the word genocide. I believe he judged the Nigerians correctly, trusting the humanity of Gowon and others. It took real, personal courage and vision on the Pope's part and I think he got it right.'

Bayer sat back as we both thought for a while. I hadn't thought of the missionaries' trauma in this way before. At the time, I had desperately wanted to be with them, to share their fate – whatever it might turn out to be. Later, I could only share the sense of hurt at the wrong they had suffered.

'Perhaps you're right, Carlo. I simply hadn't considered it quite like that. The Nigerians' emphasis was on rebuilding their community. I remember many of them saying how they feared that Biafra would be just a giant graveyard by the time they got it back. Most of them, at least, acknowledged that it was the churches' work, supported by the airlift, that prevented that. It was most encouraging, too, that people like Bishop Cockin were open in their support of them, offering to share their "honourable imprisonment". That meant a lot – and also helped to galvanise international opinion.'

Cockin had been the Anglican Bishop of Owerri and had

written a most supportive letter to the London Times challenging 'the Anglican Gowon' to consider how others might perceive his actions. His support had been both timely and heart-warming for his Catholic colleagues.

Following such international protests, the missionaries were deported. Some had been charged and tried, others just detained and deported.

'How did you feel the international reaction affected things, Carlo?'

'I've thought about that, too, Tony. On balance, I'd give the credit to the Nigerians themselves for controlling their army and for the orderly way in which the Igbos were re-integrated in Nigeria. Perhaps the diplomatic appeals of your government, mine and many others, helped, but I think the inherent decency of the Nigerians was the biggest factor. What did you think?'

'The confusion ... I suppose I remember the confusion most. Nobody knew what was happening. Princess Cecilia's graphic description of murder and rape was in sharp contrast to Lord Hunt's assertion that such reports were exaggerated and irresponsible. Nobody doubted the Princess' sincerity but people questioned whether she had access to enough information. On the other hand, people didn't trust Hunt's report because of the British government's record of propaganda and involvement in the conflict.'

Many were predicting a total massacre of the Igbos around the time the war ended. Both Princess Cecilia de Bourbon-Parma, who had sent relief supplies to Biafra, and Lord Hunt, Britain's Special Envoy, had visited Biafra to assess the situation. Hunt's report, happily, turned out to be more accurate. Relief supplies got through and thousands of displaced people returned home.

'As you say, Carlo, on balance, I agree. It was mainly the decency of the Nigerians that avoided the bloodbath. However, I think the international pressure, from governments and Protestant churches especially, had a lot to do with the speed with which the missionaries were deported rather than being held in prison. And the conditions...'

'Ja, the conditions...'

The conditions were appalling. Mercifully, the periods in jail, before their trials and afterwards before deportation, were measured in weeks. That doesn't seem much to some people, set against the risk of a catastrophic bloodbath. But, for most of them, it was a terrible trauma. They had devoted their lives to the people there, had given up their families and friends to such an extent that to leave Nigeria was heart-breaking. Many of the older missionaries just wanted to be buried in the parishes they had served.

'The way I see it, Carlo, most men, if they're fired, have a wife and family to fall back on. They have their home, famil-iar furniture... things that identify an individual. These chaps lost all of that in one fell swoop. And the trauma of the uncertainty ...'

'I remember ... Do you remember how some of them coped? Do you remember the in-service training course in theology, and the bridge school they organised for them-selves in prison?'

I smiled, and felt the tension easing in me. 'Of course. And the courtroom humour, too, despite everything!'

During one of these trials, a missionary who was well known for his sense of humour was asked by the state prosecutor: 'Do you plead guilty or not guilty to the charges of entering Nigeria unlawfully and accepting employment without the consent in writing of the Chief Federal Immigration Officer?'

The missionary amazed all present with his reply:

'Guilty, but insane.'

'Ah yes, Tony, that's how we should all plead! There was a story about Denis Foley in court, too, but I can't remember how it went.' I was delighted to remind him.

Judge Amachiri presided at one of these court proceed-ings. He was in his fifties, British-trained, and highly respected for his past achievements as a lawyer. Wearing judicial robes, he sat in a leather-covered swivel chair. Such was the public interest in the trial that the court-room was full and a few foreign embassies were represented.

The missionaries were called to the dock, one by one, and formally charged. When Father Denis Foley, a well known educator in Nigeria, was called to the dock, Judge Amachiri gazed at him in bewilderment. He beckoned him to approach the bench and, in a subdued voice, said: 'Father, I think I know you. Aren't you the priest who taught my two sons at Kalabari College?'

Denis smiled: 'That's right, my lord.'

The Judge bowed his head slightly: 'My sons told me that you're a great teacher. But this is a terrible business. I'm sorry about the trial, Father.'

Denis returned to his place in the courtroom and the trial proceeded.

Many of the officials found it difficult and painful to imprison the missionaries. They had to do it, but some of them were as gentle and considerate as they could be. I remember hearing about the elderly prison governor who spoke to a group of them before they were released for deportation. The missionaries were lined up and the governor, bowing his head and with great emotion, said something like:

'Reverend gentlemen, I would like you to understand that the task of detaining you here has been the most painful act in my thirty-five years of prison service. I ask you to understand that I had no choice in the matter. I had to do my duty.'

When I got to that point, Carlo sat forward in his chair:

'Didn't he shake hands with each of them before they left the prison? It's amazing how such a simple gesture can mean so much.'

'I agree, Carlo, and there were many more such kind gestures, but for the life of me, I couldn't understand why they had to destroy the graves at Uli. That seemed just senseless.'

Shortly after the war, the graves of 157 JCA employees at

Uli – 122 Igbo ground staff and 35 European and North American pilots, aircrew and others – were bulldozed by the Nigerian forces in an effort to obliterate the memory of Biafra. Tombstones sent by JCA were destroyed. Relatives and friends couldn't locate their loved ones' graves.

'I'm surprised at an Irishman saying that, Tony. Wasn't it Pearse who said: "The fools, the fools, they have left us our Fenian dead ..." and something about while they were there, "Ireland unfree" could never be at peace. Graves are very powerful symbols everywhere. I'm not saying they needed to destroy them, or should have, but I can understand it.'

'One of the pilots gave you a lovely poem by a Scots poet. The pilot had a Scottish name, too, I think. Can you still remember it?'

'Of course, Carlo. Skip McVitie gave it to me before we left São Tomé. That poem, by Hazel Aiken, is very precious to me. It was just what many of us needed at the time. It went:

> Perhaps you feel you have lived in vain,
> That you have failed somehow;
> But if you have touched one human heart,
> Or kept one solemn vow,
> Or brought to one sad stricken soul
> The hope to live again,
> Why then no matter how you feel
> You have not lived in vain.

Carlo was very close to tears. 'Beautiful, beautiful. Isn't that a more fitting tribute to our friends than any lump of stone ... and words cannot be destroyed.'

We sat in companionable silence for a while. Then he stood up abruptly: 'Coffee? Let's make some more coffee.'

As he made the coffee, we spoke about the amazing generosity of people who contributed forty million pounds through thirty-five church organisations in twenty-one countries and about the phenomenal effect of television and the extraordinary kindnesses that it prompted from ordinary individuals.

He poured the coffee, then stood still, the coffee-pot still raised:

'At least Ojukwu got one thing right when he was in exile. You remember he said that they had always believed in the futility of the war, that they had always maintained that the war would solve no problems.'

He was quiet for a while. We knew each other so well that I could sense he was building himself up to say something even more extraordinary. I made myself relax quietly and wait for him to continue.

A few minutes later, he broke the silence:

'Tony, I only partly answered that student earlier about the causes of this war. I said that the colonial issue was the difficult one.

'Empires and dictators have one thing in common. They suppress local differences and conflicts. I'm afraid that as each country embraces democracy, these conflicts will spill out as they did in Nigeria. Tribal jealousies, religious differences, old grudges of one sort or another that were suppressed by dictators or outsiders will re-emerge.

'I hope I'm wrong, but I think it will happen in many parts of Africa and in Europe, too, if Eastern Europe returns to democracy. Unfortunately, I think it may be a price that will have to be paid for democracy. The alternative is worse, in my opinion. I think, in time, people will see just how moderate and sensible the Nigerians have been.'

'Don't forget we had a civil war in Ireland, too. I can remember the legacy of bitterness...'

'I'm sorry, Tony, of course. You'll understand that it takes time to heal but do you remember the enthusiasm with which the new Nigeria greeted its independence, the harmony, the dreams of nation-building? They all shared those dreams before it turned sour. Tribal distrust runs deep, and it'll take a long time for any African nation to merge into a homogeneous union.

'In time they will. In another generation, Nigeria will be

able to face its history, to talk openly about Biafra and the role of its civil war in making a modern Nigerian state. They must be challenged to do so, then. They responded magnificently to the Pope's challenge and I believe they'll respond well to another, when the time is right. It would be a demonstration of their maturity as a nation to acknowledge their history, build a monument at Uli and acknowledge the roles of all the participants in the tragedy.'

'Hold on, Carlo. I agree they should, of course, but why on earth would they respond to such a challenge?'

'When the time comes, the Nigerians will respond because it'll suit them, they'll be ready to do so – and they'll know it's right!'

There were so many other topics we wanted to talk about but, at two in the morning, we decided to leave them for another night.

We didn't get another opportunity, so that those two nights, in Rome and in Vienna, will be forever twinned in my memory.

CHAPTER 9

Hopeville

The market place at Uturu looked busy to casual observers. Only those who had known it before the war would have realised how sparsely stocked the stalls were. The stall-holders still wore bright-coloured clothes, but the more observant could see that they were not quite as bright as they had been. The bright dyes were fading now in clothes that had been washed many times and patched too often. Nobody had money to buy anything.

After the war, the Biafran currency had been frozen. It was worthless now. Everything was bartered, even by the Nigerian soldiers who would have to wait for their pay until they returned to their home barracks. In the meantime, they traded some of the clothes and other things they had taken as booty for palm wine or other luxuries.

The stall-holders and their regular customers did complicated deals for fresh produce and second-hand clothes – or anything else that was available. One stall-holder 'sold' slices of boiled yam. That was the only food that could be bought, ready to eat, in the market every day. Before the war, hard-boiled eggs had been popular but chickens had all been more urgently needed for the pot when food became scarce.

Near the entrance to the market, four young men sat trying to catch the eyes of passers-by as they begged for their needs. They were willing to work, but what could one-legged men do when there were plenty of able-bodied young men looking for any work that was available.

When the war started, Nick Ahaji had been one of the first to join up. He had been proud when he got one of the few

AK 47s. His friends had said he was sure to be promoted when he got the powerful gun. Many conscripts who came later had only a machete with which to fight the Nigerians.

The captain encouraged all the young soldiers, assuring them that they were always looking for 'officer material'. Nick had worked hard, doing unpopular duties willingly, in the hope that Major Okpara, a very fair man, might recommend him for promotion. He had not seen Okpara again after Calabar, more's the pity.

In the hectic battles and skirmishes which followed the fall of Calabar, he had distinguished himself many times. A few officers had told him they would mention him in their dispatches. He often wondered if they did – before his right leg was shattered in that furious skirmish near Ikang.

The doctors had done their best at the hospital, but it had been a terrible moment when they told him that it would have to be amputated. When he left the hospital, he had been too ashamed, at first, to return to Uturu. Maybe, in a strange place, it would be easier to adjust. He winced as he remembered those few weeks before he made his way painfully home.

His sister Elizabeth had been wonderful, welcoming him with open arms. Somehow, they had survived until her husband Peter came home. Things had improved a little then but he feared that Peter might not understand. A few nights later, Peter reassured him: 'Don't worry, brother, I do understand. Any of us could have lost a leg. We've many shared experiences from the war. Now we'll share the pot, each of us putting in what we can. We'll manage.'

That was good but he knew they had little enough and he was desperate to contribute his share, especially now that Elizabeth was expecting a baby.

A young woman came by with a basket on her head. She seemed different and they smiled at her, hopefully. So many others looked quickly away. In a deft movement, she swung the basket from her head, slipping it under her arm. She handed a paw-paw, with a smile, to Ahaji.

Three Nigerian soldiers came over to them. The corporal was a lot older than the others. He looked a tough one, but had a gentle voice: 'Good morning. How are you? We'd trouble during the war from you rebels. Many of our men got injuries like your own. Where were you injured, what front?'

Ahaji replied quickly: 'Well sir, I lost my leg at Ikang, Joseph lost his at Enugu and the others lost theirs at Ikot Ene.'

'Where are these Ikang and Ikot Ene places?'

'Near Calabar, sir. They're really just villages.'

'The smaller battles were often the fiercest...'

The corporal had a far away expression that Ahaji knew well. After a moment, he turned back to them and smiled:

'Here, brothers, take these kola nuts. You're welcome.'

As the soldiers strolled off, Ahaji felt they were the ones who understood, former enemies or not.

Early one morning a van drew up and a man in white missionary garb got out. He leant in to the passenger seat and took out a small bundle of shirts. As he came near the four veterans, Ahaji thought he looked familiar, but it was only when he greeted them that Ahaji was sure:

'Good morning men.'

Ahaji stared at the missionary in astonishment:

'Hey, Br Frank! It's great to see you again. Do you recognise me, Nicholas Ahaji? You taught me in school. What brings you to the market? If you want to sell those shirts, I'll make sure you get the very best price.'

'I'm sorry, Nicholas, I didn't recognise you at first, but I remember you now. Sorry to see you've lost a leg, but it's good to see you. What I'm really looking for is a tough, hard-working man to help us with some building. He'll have to work with us for a year or so and he'll have to be strong.'

Nick reached for his home-made crutches, starting to get up to help Frank.

'There are plenty of good men who'd like to work with you. I know them all and I'll help you find a good man.'

Frank held Nick's eyes. His voice was quiet but steady:

'The man I'm looking for will be a veteran with great courage, who will be prepared to help other veterans after he has learnt a trade with us. In a year's time, he'll have to come back here and lead others, inspire them with hope. He probably only has one leg and we hope that together we can make him an artificial one, so that he can walk back in here next year. Are you that man, Nicholas?'

For a moment the world swam. Ahaji thought he must be dreaming but Frank never asked anyone to do the impossible. Nearly impossible, maybe. He looked at Frank, his eyes showing excitement now:

'I'll do it! I promise you I'll do my very best and won't let you down. A new leg... Whatever it takes, I'll do it.'

'That's the stuff. Can you be ready, here, next Monday to meet the van?''

'Of course, and thanks, I'll wait here.'

Impulsively, Frank took three of the shirts from the small bundle and handed one to each:

'When you wear these, you'll remember his promise. Nicholas will soon make his own shirts!'

Nick laughed:

'You haven't changed, Br Frank! I'm glad.'

The following Monday morning, before the market opened, Ahaji was waiting. Elizabeth and Peter had come with him, helping him to carry his belongings. He had few clothes but, at least, he had his own blanket. A small bag held his clothes and a contribution of food towards the pot in his new home – a few yams, some cassava and green greens that Elizabeth added.

Shortly after the market opened, his three veteran friends arrived, each wearing his new shirt proudly. They spoke excitedly to him, wishing him well and assuring him that they would be ready to help him when he returned.

'My friends, you must start to work before that. Find out

everything there is to be known about shirts and trousers. We'll be the best tailors in Nigeria, soon. There's no money, no cloth now – but there will be. You must be able to tell me what cloth there is, the type of clothes and colours that people want and you must know the best prices for everything. That way, when I get back you'll know what we should make.'

One of the traders came over to him and embraced him: 'Nick, good luck and go well! Your friends have told us about Br Frank. You should bring him a special dash – a present from all of us to thank him. Here is some sugar. Give it to him when you reach the mission.'

The traders nearby were clapping. It seemed the whole market knew that he was going, wanted to share his joy. As he thanked them, he chuckled at the thought of the bartering that must have gone into getting this bag of sugar. He hadn't thought there was any left in Nigeria – well, in Biafra anyhow.

A short while later, the van drew up and he said his good-byes.

Frank greeted the veterans and he was struck by the change in their faces from just a few days ago. He prayed that he hadn't built up their hopes unreasonably. It would be cruel to disappoint them. There were thousands who needed new legs to cope with their disabilities and skills to earn a living. He could only help a handful.

As they drove to the mission, Nick wondered about his new companions: 'Are there many more like me at the mission, Brother?'

'Just eight men, at the moment, Nick. You'll be the ninth but there'll soon be another hundred. We're building new houses to accommodate them and then we'll really get going. I want us to start as we intend to go on, with as much work as possible done by veterans, amputees like yourself.

'We started with a few men, just trying to teach them a skill. Then, one day, John Amanze arrived, walking on a peg-leg – a wooden piece tied to his leg stump – that he had made himself. It wasn't very good, but he was terribly proud of it, and rightly so. He inspired us to try to make something better. It will take time but we will, Nick, we will.'

'It's great to feel part of something, again, Brother. It'd be wonderful to say "I made my own leg", or played a part in it. Anything would be better than just sitting in that market for the rest of our lives. But to share in the work, to be able to say that we helped to make it happen. Hey! That would be wonderful. I could never thank you enough.'

Frank laughed: 'You mightn't thank me when you realise how tough it's going to be. Anyhow, we've got some money from a German Catholic group called Misereor, now. They've given us enough to build the accommodation and workshops, pay for machines, equipment and the basic materials we need. They've made it possible but together we'll have to make it happen.'

'I assure you, I'll... No, we'll all work to make it happen. Any man that needs help or encouragement, we'll help him if he tries his best. If anyone won't try, he'll answer to the rest of us. No one'll let you down, I promise.'

'You haven't met them yet, Nick.'

'In the fighting, I think I met all kinds. You soon understand each other in a battle – the men you can trust, the one who needs help, the one who's selfish. They're all there.'

Frank was astonished at the young man. There was no hint of bitterness and he felt sure he was no bully, just a man determined to grasp the opportunity and to help others to do so. He smiled to himself as he wondered, not for the first time, who was encouraging whom.

With such determination they couldn't fail.

He turned to Nick again: 'I'd like to call the project "Hopeville" but I don't think we should use the name until we have men walking on legs that we've made ourselves. We mustn't raise hopes unfairly. What do you think, Nick?'

'Yes, I agree. That is very good. Hopeville would be a wonderful name, though, and I feel it'll soon be possible. If others can make legs and walk on them, why can't we?'

For a month after Ahaji's arrival at the mission, the work was
very hard as the small number of men struggled to finish off
the buildings. In the process they were learning new skills
from the few able-bodied tradesmen and the brothers. As the
new men arrived, 140 of them, they were amazed at what
their fellow amputees had been able to do.

Shortly after they arrived, Frank spoke to them all:

'Greetings! You're all welcome to your new home for the
next year. When you leave here then, we want you to take
three things with you: new legs, new skills to earn your own
living and new hope to face the future. That hope is the most
important thing you will take away. To earn it, you must take
responsibility for as much as possible yourselves. For the first
month, until you know each other, we brothers will make the
decisions. Then you must elect your own leaders, a council
through which you'll make your own decisions and take responsibility for yourselves.'

'Tomorrow you'll start to learn your new skills, in classes
and in practical work. At first you'll try different things until
we can decide together which training would most suit each
individual.'

'New legs will take time. In the meantime you must learn
to use the one you have better, make yourselves fitter so that
you'll be strong enough to use the new leg when your turn
comes. I want you to try to devise some sports activities that
you can do and enjoy to help you improve your strength and
fitness. I know you'll all do your best.'

'We'll talk more again.'

They clapped and cheered him with enthusiasm. Here,
they knew they could feel at home.

The following day Ahaji was disappointed to find he had
been allocated to book-keeping classes. There were just too
many for the tailoring group that, by now, he really wanted.
Others were learning carpentry, shoemaking, radio and clock
repairs, waxing, silver-smithing and rabbit rearing.

He refused to be discouraged though, and set about learning as much as he could. He hated the book-keeping but
acknowledged to himself that it might be useful. In the
evenings, when others grumbled, he would tell them, bluntly:
'I'd much rather work, even as a book-keeper, than spend the
rest of my life begging in the market.'

When some of them suggested that they try to play football,
he was sceptical but agreed to try. Soon, they started to adjust
the rules to take account of their handicap. Deliberately knocking an opponent's crutch became an automatic penalty, no
matter where it happened on the field. As a player, he wasn't
much good, but the others often asked him to act as referee.

They tried many athletic events. It surprised everyone
that the high jump became the most popular event. Ahaji
tried them all. He was always one of the most enthusiastic –
but usually nearly last. Nothing could spoil his enthusiasm,
however, and he always encouraged everyone else.

Everyone was delighted when he was elected committee
secretary. That key role needed his enthusiasm and capacity
for hard work. Eight of the original 149 men had left, unable
to cope with the strenuous routine. When three more left,
Nick was furious, feeling they had let everyone down. He
discussed it with Frank, suggesting that they had broken
their promise and that action would have to be taken to stop
any more leaving.

Frank was very gentle:

'Nick, you've all suffered more than just the pain of losing
your leg. The trauma of your loss is also serious. Some can
cope better than others but many will need a lot of time to
come to terms with their loss, to adjust. We must be patient
and give each man the time he needs. Actually, I was afraid
we would have lost more, by now.'

'I don't understand, what do you mean by this "trauma"?'

'Well Nick, I don't fully understand it myself. I'm not a
doctor, but all of us were shocked by the war, even those who
were just here, not involved in any battles. Most of you went

through much worse experiences. Some can cope, some need time and a few will never cope, like the "combat boys".'

'I worked with alcoholics for years and I can tell you that many men need a lot of time to come to terms with their problems. We must encourage them, if we can, but give each man the time he needs.'

The working groups had changed around many times. Nick was now firmly established in the tailoring class and had already made himself a shirt. It wasn't very good, really, but, even after he had made himself much better ones, Nick still wore that shirt with fierce pride. Many years later, he would still put it on occasionally – just to remind himself how it had all started. Much more important, though, was the progress with the artificial legs. John Amanze was now walking reasonably well on the first leg they had made, his peg-leg almost forgotten. He still liked the nickname 'Long John', though, and he took great pride in the fact that it was his first crude effort that had inspired the project.

The first attempts at making artificial limbs were far from sophisticated. The local carvers had used pieces of wood to make legs and feet. Then they hollowed out the top of the wooden legs sufficiently to allow the amputees' stumps to fit in as comfortably as possible.

With the help of spongy material cut from the soles of flip-flop sandals, the craftsmen and women made ankle joints. They used hubs from old bicycle wheels to make knee joints. Strips of elastic were put on the artificial feet to give them some leverage. Elastic strips were also attached from the thighs to the heels to facilitate the forward and return movement of the artificial limb.

With each attempt, the engineering skill and the comfort improved, as both the local craftsmen and the amputees themselves added their suggestions. When Jan Gainer was appointed to the project, the quality improved further. She was a qualified physiotherapist, a CUSO volunteer from

Canada. Jan was able to make great improvements to the design, to the taking of measurements and to the skills involved in fitting them. Her training and her patience were invaluable as she taught the men to use their strange new limbs.

At that time, in Europe, it cost seventy pounds to buy a mechanical leg and professional fitting services cost many times the price of the limb. Hopeville could make one for seven pounds. Jan fitted them, with the help of some volunteers from the amputees themselves.

Nick was just starting to have his leg fitted. Through the following weeks, Jan patiently measured everything, working with the carvers to make all the appropriate minor adjustments until it fitted comfortably. Nick could hardly restrain himself with excitement.

When the great day came and he finally tried to walk on the leg, he fell many times. Jan was always there and patiently encouraged him to work his way along the parallel bars and back again. Some days, it seemed, her main role was to discourage Nick from doing too much, too soon.

After about a week, Jan gave Nick a warm hug: 'Right, Nick, I think you're ready to try walking without the bars.'

For the first time Nick was unsure but he had great trust in Jan. As she handed him the walking stick, Nick held her hand tightly:

'You just tell me what to do, Jan. Please don't let me do too little, or too much.'

Within another week he no longer needed the walking stick – just, as Jan had told him, 'lots of practice'.

About that time, the wood-working class gave Frank a board with the name 'Hopeville' carefully carved on it. As soon as Long John was able to walk comfortably on his new leg, Frank confidently erected the board and the project officially took on its new name.

The year had rolled by very quickly. A total of 39 out of the original 149 had dropped out at different stages, unable to take the pressure. Frank had spoken to each of them, encouraging them and saying that when they were ready they should consider trying again. To Nick and others who argued that they'd had their chance, he explained that anyone who came back a second time would know what to expect. Given a second chance, they'd be much less likely to drop out.

The 110 who were left were all now proficient at their chosen skills and growing steadily in confidence, making plans for their future and assuring Frank that they would honour their promise to him to help others.

For the past month they had been working confidently on their own tools and equipment. These they would take home with them, to their own towns and villages, to help them earn a living.

Nick was very proud of his new sewing machine. By now, it seemed as familiar as his right arm or, indeed, his new right leg. He was no longer sure which he prized most and glad that he didn't have to chose.

At 25 years of age, he was the oldest 'veteran' from the war and from the tough grind of the rehabilitation programme.

All that remained was the graduation ceremony.

The cathedral in Enugu was full to capacity with a large congregation that included the relatives and friends of the graduates. Bishop Godfrey Okoye would preside over the Mass and the graduation ceremony. The 110 amputees who had completed this first programme came up the aisle of the cathedral on crutches, with their new legs slung over their shoulders. At the altar, Bishop Okoye blessed the limbs.

After the Bishop's blessing and address, the graduates went to the sacristy on crutches, where they fitted on their artificial limbs. They left their crutches in the sacristy and returned to the cathedral walking tall down the aisle, to take their seats. Everyone cheered and applauded with joy.

It was a most moving experience for the hundreds who participated. Hopeville was an extraordinarily apt name.

After the ceremony, Nick met Peter and Elizabeth with their new baby. When they had greeted each other, Nick was proud to hold baby Frank with both arms, no longer hindered by the crutch.

Elizabeth could hardly speak, she was so happy.

'Nick, we've prepared a small feast to celebrate your homecoming. Our friends and neighbours in the village want to share in your joy and your achievement. They'll have everything prepared for when we arrive.'

Nick smiled at her:

'Yes, we'll enjoy that together and thank you, but first, I must take a little walk down to the market-place.'

Epilogue

The war ended on Monday, 12 January 1970.

Casseroli and Gallina had met Bayer and I just two days before that. As the news unfolded rapidly, that Saturday night in Bayer's apartment was the only time I had to reflect on the thirty-one months of bitter conflict.

The next morning, Sunday, Pope Paul devoted his normal weekly address in St Peter's Square to the impending end of the war. His carefully measured challenge, his appeal 'on bended knees' to avoid genocide was made just a few hours before Uli airstrip was captured.

Later that day, Fr Tom Cunningham flew with Captain Johnsonn and an Icelandic crew in a spirited attempt to use an airstrip at Ugah to get in further medical supplies. The facilities were poor and they had just unloaded their cargo when the Nigerian forces began to overrun the airstrip. In the ensuing panic, soldiers and civilians scrambled on board the JCA aircraft. Johnsonn had to take off in a hurry, with the cargo door still open, as the plane was hit repeatedly by machine-gun fire. The door sheared off in mid-flight, adding to the fear in the crowded plane. They were lucky to get back to São Tomé, at all.

That was the last JCA flight.

Emergency programmes are never easy to phase out. Bayer had been through it all before and understood the meticulous planning that was needed. Action could not be allowed to be paralysed by emotion or discussions about what should or shouldn't have happened.

The children in São Tomé had to be helped gently to realise that they were now Nigerians, not Biafrans. The country they had come from no longer existed. The rehabilitation programme would have to be carefully planned. The hospital building should be donated to São Tomé, the equipment and medical supplies given to some needy hospital elsewhere. The planes and the rest of the airlift structure must be dispersed as soon as possible. The toughest problem of all was to dispose of the thousands of tons of food in São Tomé. Nigeria wouldn't accept it.

These were serious problems but the one that preoccupied me was the safety of the missionaries and local church personnel. There was no news of them. Bayer was confident about their safety, though, certain that the Nigerians wouldn't want the condemnation of the international community. Apart from anything else, they needed a lot of international money to rebuild the country.

On the Wednesday morning, as soon as Bayer and I arrived in the Caritas office, he took off his jacket as usual, rolled up his shirt sleeves and was in full swing. He lifted a file marked 'Angola' and gave it to me.

'Read this, Tony. Tell me what you think.'

Bayer left the office and I tried to concentrate on the file. I felt he was being kind, distracting me from my concern for my friends in Biafra, former Biafra, I corrected myself. Caritas Angola were looking for help in assisting 80,000 refugees in camps and the Portuguese government was willing to co-operate. In an early margin note, Bayer had wondered whether they were refugee or concentration camps. By the time I had finished reading the file, I was no nearer answering that question.

Bayer came back to the room and smiled: 'Well?'

'I just don't know, Carlo.'

He smiled again: 'You'd better go to Luanda, then, and find out! TAP have a direct flight from Lisbon tomorrow morning. I'll cable ahead.'

When I protested, Bayer's reply was blunt but typical of him: 'Tony, there's always a crisis, people who need help. We can't afford to look back.

'Life goes on, my friend.'

* * *

Life does go on and every tragedy passes. A pond will close over the biggest stone that's tossed into it. When the splash has gone, though, the ripples can be seen for a long time – the beauty remaining, the disturbance gone. Biafra had no shortage of heroes and heroines who rose nobly above the horrors of the war. People like the 'mamas' who stood up to the gun-toting young men, and Ahaji, who displayed another type of fortitude.

In world terms, Biafra was a small pond indeed but the ripples from that conflict still have a good effect all over Africa, in Asia, the Americas and Europe. As Bayer said in Vienna, it seems as if Nigeria's loss, when they deported the missionaries, has been everyone else's gain.

P. J. O'Connor and Augustine O'Keeffe planted a few seeds and grew crops at Spadeville. That helped to inspire Frank McGovern with Hopeville. When there were no more amputees who needed Hopeville, it became a centre for handicapped children and Frank returned to Ireland. Frank and his colleagues brought hope to the amputees. Now he uses that experience to bring the same hope to alcoholics in Ireland.

The missionaries who were deported continue to promote development, justice and peace, all over the globe. They manage programmes to provide relief in natural and man-made disaster areas, raise funds for self-reliance projects and give counselling and support to the victims of many tragedies.

Many missionaries say that their Biafran experience inspired their work. They often speak of how much they learned from Biafra and from the Igbo people as they shared with them that troubled period in Nigeria's history. That learning process continues as they join with others, or others join them, in a multiplicity of projects. The ripples continue...

Some concentrated on ecumenical work, building on the experience of Joint Church Aid. It was a landmark organisation, marking the most significant co-operation between the Christian churches, giving witness of a new and better understanding of our common Christianity, working together and with secular organisations to feed the hungry. The work still continues, as some of the former missionaries try to break down the barriers of misunderstanding with those who follow Islam and other faiths.

Raymond Kennedy, one of the three priests who persuaded the pilots flying military supplies to carry food parcels, was a Diocesan Director of Ecumenism in California before establishing a Christian-Muslim teacher training college in Bangladesh.

Fintan Kilbride and Dermot Doran, the other two who persuaded the pilots, are both in Canada. Fintan helps Vietnamese boat people there and Dermot administers the flourishing Volunteer International Christian Service. A new generation of young volunteers from VICS carry on the traditions, sharing experiences as well as caring, carrying the flame of hope back and forth across frontiers and continents to Africa and elsewhere – and back again.

These three, Raymond, Fintan and Dermot, could never have dreamed that their early television appeals would have had the effect they had. It has been wonderful to see top professional entertainers get behind the message for Ethiopia, Rwanda and other disaster areas.

The personal connections are always fascinating. Raymond and the two Doheny brothers, Kevin and Michael, sought the support of their families and friends for their work in the airlift. The response was so enthusiastic that Africa Concern was founded by the Kennedys, the Dohenys and their friends.

Concern, as an organisation, grew directly from a simple appeal for famine relief to Biafra, called SOS – Send One Ship.

Now there are Concern Worldwide, its headquarters still in Dublin, Concern Universal in the UK, and Concern America. Today, Concern Worldwide operates mainly in ten African and four Asian countries, through two hundred volunteers and six thousand local staff. Over the years there have been two thousand volunteers – professional and skilled workers. Its annual contribution to relief programmes rivals the official aid budgets of some small nations.

Aengus and Jack Finucane, now executives with Concern, gained their early experience of relief operations the hard way, at Uli airstrip and in the feeding centres. As a result, they can now offer a wealth of experience to their colleagues and co-workers.

The Church Relief and Development Association in Ethiopia (CRDA) was founded by Kevin Doheny and has been directed by Augustine O'Keeffe, who had been in Spadeville. CRDA has 106 member organisations. Kevin and other ex-Nigerian volunteers established the International Refugee Trust in the UK and the Refugee Trust in Ireland. Currently, the Refugee Trusts are active in Bosnia, Turkey, Rwanda, Kenya, Sierra Leone and Guinea.

Some ripples indeed...

... and, of course, they're all needed. There are about 40 million refugees in the world, right now. The power of hope recognises no frontiers.

Pastor Viggo Mollerup enjoys a well-earned retirement in Copenhagen.

Count Carl Von Rosen was again involved in relief work when he was killed in a rocket attack on Ogaden in 1977. Larry Rabb is still flying in America, Butch Dutting semi-retired...

... and those who returned to being parish priests – among them Tom Cunningham in England, Bill Butler, Joe Prendergast and Desmond McGlade in the United States... the people of Uli are unlikely to forget 'Glade'.

Bayer died in 1977, following a heart attack. His grave is

adjacent to St Peter's Square, in Rome, amongst the graves of many of the other monsignori with whom he argued and debated policy. The two people he served have also died, Pope Paul VI in 1978 and Cardinal Benelli in 1982.

Archbishop Arinze played a key role in restructuring the Nigerian church after the departure of the missionaries. Now, he's a cardinal in Rome, one of a handful regularly named as 'papabile', possibly a future Pope.

The departure of the missionaries expedited the Africanisation of the church and the local church continued the good work to the great joy, but far beyond the expectations, of their former colleagues. Many Igbo church personnel are now missionaries elsewhere in Africa, in Europe and in North America.

General Gowon was deposed in a bloodless coup in 1975 and now lives in England. Colonel Ojukwu is back in Nigeria, and active in local politics.

If you need a good suit, Nicholas Ahaji and Co would be glad to oblige!

* * *

It was much later, twenty-four years after the end of the war in fact, that Harry Mullin was invited to attend the centenary celebration of the parish where he served in former Biafra. It was a most joyful occasion. Every street in the village was decorated with palm branches. There was a carnival atmosphere, in true African style.

People were singing everywhere. Old and young alike joined in the dances, clapping and stamping. They created a vibrant, pulsing beat, one that could be heard by every muscle and sinew in the body.

As the car approached the centre of the village, it slowed down and Harry was fascinated that he could recognise and remember not just the houses, but their fruit trees as well. There were some changes, of course, some new houses and others where the trees had been cleared to build a carport.

That old mango tree was still lording it over everything!
On impulse, he turned to the young man who was driving:
'Do you remember making a toy thurible, Moses?'
'Ah now, Fr Harry, we made lots of things as kids.'
'I know, but I remember Joseph and yourself with that one
as if it were yesterday! An old milk tin, some twine and plenty of
imagination!'
Moses's wife, Sarah, chuckled: 'You must tell me more. I
love this village but I find it very hard to get Moses to tell me
anything about it, or about when he was a child.'
Harry had been delighted when Moses and his wife
collected him at Enugu airport. The little 'Chief', as he
would always think of Moses, was a successful lawyer in
Enugu now and Sarah was from the city.
'Early tomorrow morning, I'll be sitting under that old
mango tree and, I suppose, remembering. I always loved
watching the children play. If you're there, I'll tell you everything about the village as it was thirty years ago, before the
war – and a lot about Moses, that he doesn't remember!'
They were all laughing as Sarah replied:
'It's a date... it's so tranquil there, I could sit there for hours.'
Moses parked the car and ushered Harry to the stage that
had been erected for the celebrations. There, the traditional
leaders had their places of honour.
The elders installed Harry as a chief, dressed him in traditional robes and gave him the title Chief Ozo Ndu I (Chief
Life Saver I) which was a cultural honour of tremendous
importance.
There were many speeches of welcome for Harry, inter-
spersed with more music and dancing. Then, one by one the
people came, said a few words of welcome and presented
gifts. A young and beautiful-looking woman came on the
stage. She wore a multi-coloured ankle-length dress with an
elegant head-dress to match. Her face glowed with delight as
she presented a silver plate with her gift on it. She spoke in a
clear voice, through the microphone:

'Reverend Father, Chief Ozo Ndu I ...'

Her voice was drowned by the cheers and the applause of the crowd. The master of ceremonies asked for silence and beckoned to the young woman to continue her address...

'You're welcome back to our parish. You are our father and we receive you as such. During the war, I was dying of starvation and you sent me and many other young children to São Tomé, where we were treated. Before I left this parish you put a wrist-band on me so that I would be easily identified. You wrote my name on it with special ink. I want you to accept that wrist-band now as a reminder of all the children you saved.'

'These children have become healthy adults. Today you can see many of us standing around this stage with our own children. The children want to sing a special song of thanks to you for saving their parents' lives.'

Harry tried to choke back his tears as he thanked the lady for the treasured gift which no money could buy. As the group of little children sang their song, Harry looked at the name on the wrist-band. Through his tears, he looked back at the beautiful woman, trying to recognise Lucy, the little girl who had cried during the hunger strike at the hospital in São Tomé.

Chief Moses had banned 'that black stuff' and they had all followed him. It really was Lucy Eke, smiling in front of him, as the children danced.